Enjoy
—
inJoy

With our love
Geeco

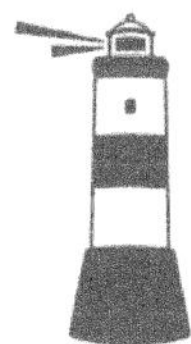

Geeco Publishing

First Published Amazon Kindle 2020

www.geecopublishing.com

ISBN: 978 1 5272 7823 3

Disclaimer

The advice and strategies found within may not be suitable for every situation. This work is sold with the understanding that neither the author nor the publisher are held responsible for the results accrued from the advice in this book.

Also published by Geeco – A Simple Way

Tradition 12

"Anonymity is the spiritual foundation of all our traditions, ever reminding us to place principles before personalities."

This book has been created by the joint efforts of the members of Geeco, and we are equal creators, we offer it to you from our collective name of Geeco.

You can communicate with us at geeco909@gmail.com

If you enjoy the messages in this book, help us to get them out there by leaving a review on Amazon.

Enjoy

January 1

Sorry

'Amazing how many people are sorry for the consequences they suffer as a result of their terrible actions, yet completely unremorseful with regard to the ones they intentionally harmed by those same actions.'

Ken Poirot

'I'm sorry' I used to say, with my eyes downcast, my back slightly bent, the child in me still expecting punishment. Punishment because I had done it again. Sorry, because somewhere deep inside, I knew I was ineffectual, though I didn't want to admit it to myself or anyone else.

Sorry, because I knew that I was actually incapable of changing the way I behaved. I had no skills – Oh yes – don't get me wrong – I had skills. I was successful, or I appeared to be successful to the world.

But where it mattered, with the ones I loved and with myself I was impotent with ineffectuality. Now you may have read that and thought, "Well, I'm not that bad."

But nearly all of us have areas in our lives where we fall way short in our behaviours towards ourselves and others and saying 'I'm sorry' is about the most ineffectual action of them all.

Really the worst thing about saying, 'I'm sorry...' is that we should not even be saying, 'I'm sorry for what I've done'. If we had any honesty (some hope of that) we would be saying, 'I'm sorry, I'm going to do it again.'

So unless we are ready to change, saying, 'I'm sorry' is about as much use as giving someone a maggot-infested piece of meat.

'Would "Sorry" have made any difference? Does it ever? It's just a word. One word against a thousand actions.'

Sarah Ockler

January 2

Happiness

'If only we'd stop trying to be happy, we could have a pretty good time.'

Edith Wharton

Happiness is a by-product of the things we do. It is not, and it cannot be a goal in its own right. If we want to be happy, we are asking for something that cannot exist without the things that created it.

So to achieve happiness, we want to know what we want and then move towards it. Being with friends can make us happy, but ultimately just being with them is not enough.

We want to choose a path that brings light into our lives and even more importantly into the lives of others.

'To be without some of the things you want is an indispensable part of happiness.'

Bertrand Russell

'But a lifetime of happiness! No man alive could bear it: it would be hell on earth.'

George Bernard Shaw

January 3

Love

'The affirmation of one's own life, happiness, growth, freedom is rooted in one's capacity to love, i.e. in care, respect, responsibility, and knowledge. If an individual is able to love productively, he loves himself too; if he can only love others, he cannot love at all.'

Erich Fromm

We need to respect and take care of ourselves. We want to love ourselves, and this doesn't just mean looking at ourselves in shop windows, it means realising that we are worthwhile, significant human beings. We need to be looked after and nourished – and if we don't do that to ourselves, then however much others may try to do it to us, they will fail.

We want to be okay to be us, to be proud of ourselves, to accept ourselves whatever our shortcomings may be. Then, and only then, are we in a position to reach out genuinely and to help and to love others.

If we hate ourselves, we may go through the motions of helping and loving others, but everybody they and we, know at some level, that it's fake.

If we have difficulty accepting ourselves, then it is worth remembering that millions of others have that difficulty too. Whatever happens, whatever we may have been through, the inner spark of love and light is still within us. We want to acknowledge it.

'What will survive us is love.'

Philip Larkin

January 4

Action

'If you think you are too small to be effective, you have never been in a bed with a mosquito.'

Betty Reese

We often shy away from opportunities and from taking action. There are times when doing nothing may be the right choice. However, there are times when we really do feel that we should do something, and yet some little voice, thought or feeling prevents us.

We can't quite take the step that would propel us into action.

And the little things we do not dare to do accumulate, and so as we go through our lives they mount up, and however successful we have been in some areas, there is still that nagging feeling of having failed, somewhere, somehow.

And so, realising that now, we may choose to change the way we react to opportunities in the future.

If we want to...

'An avalanche begins with a snowflake.'

Joseph Compton

January 5

Growth

'We can lift ourselves out of ignorance, we can find ourselves as creatures of excellence and intelligence and skill.'

Richard Bach

When we say, he did the best he could, what we really we mean is that he didn't do it badly considering.

And so the notion of doing the best we can is connected to low achievement, rather than with excellent performance.

'Vision without action is merely a dream. Action without vision just passes the time. Visions with action can change the world.'

Joel Arthur Barker

'We were born to go as far as we can fly and turn electric dreams into reality.'

Sean Allman

January 6

Anger

'Never wrestle with pigs. You both get dirty and the pig likes it.'

George Bernard Shaw

Way back when, a white American asked a Native American what he thought about white men. 'We think you are mad. Why are you so angry?'

So many people march through their lives, carrying a bubble of anger, and a basket full of opinions. 'All politicians are... All Christians are... All Muslims are... All blacks are... All whites are... All criminals are... '

Some of us temper our bigotry so that it's almost unnoticeable to us or others. Still, if we were honest, we would probably (possibly) recognise that we group and belittle people. If we had a bad experience with a banker, an estate agent, a tele-salesperson, a hospital porter, a policeman, we can suddenly we find ourselves taking against the whole group.

It might be worth realising that we are all imperfect human beings. And we all need space and love to grow and develop.

'I'm selfish, impatient and a little insecure. I make mistakes. I am out of control at times and at times hard to handle. But if you can't handle me at my worst, then you sure as hell don't deserve me at my best.'

Marilyn Monroe

January 7

Adventure

'Life is either a daring adventure or nothing. Security does not exist in nature, nor do the children of man as a whole experience it. Avoiding danger is no safer in the long run than outright exposure. The fearful are caught as often as the bold.'

Helen Keller

We live in a nanny state, suffocated by precautions.

Our children play in only 10% of the area that we played in as children.

Someone covered in bandages can't move. Worse still they can't experience, they can't breathe the air and fill their lungs with freedom.

Discard your shackles and throw caution to the wind. Go out, live, experience. Encourage your friends, your children, your parents, to do the same.

Walk out of the darkness, bathe in the light.

Choose one thing now that you will do today, that you have not done for ages or ever.

'The chief danger in life is that you may take too many precautions.'

Alfred Adler

January 8

Conscience

'My conscience hath a thousand several tongues,
And every tongue brings in a several tale,
And every tale condemns me for a villain.'

William Shakespeare – Richard III

If we lived in a house with dry rot, and we did nothing, the dry rot would continue to spread its tendrils and destroy the house.

If we have deeds, hidden from others, in our minds, they too continue to spread their evil throughout our being.

Catholics take confession – to cleanse their souls.

In AA, they admit to themselves, to their God and another human being the exact nature of their wrongs.

If we are carrying deeds that trouble us, it is well worth telling another human being, to free ourselves of their burden. It stops our conscience from stabbing us and dragging us down.

'Silent anguish is the more dangerous.'

Jean Racine

'A peace above all earthly dignities,
A still and quiet conscience.'

William Shakespeare – Henry VIII

January 9

Resentments

'How much more grievous are the consequences of anger than the causes of it.'

Marcus Aurelius

Whether our anger, resentments or irritations are justified or not, we are the ones who are hurt by them.

They are nooses around our necks, that choke our freedom. They are gaping wounds through which our lifeblood squirts, leaving us bereft.

To regain peace of mind, we want to forgive anyone whom we think has caused us harm.

We choose how we react to what has been done. Only we are responsible for our feelings.

When we forgive, we should not feel self-righteous, because if we do, we are not forgiving.

When we forgive and move on, we can be grateful for the spiritual path that we are enjoying.

'But I do nothing upon myself, and yet I am my own Executioner.'

John Donne

January 10

Isolation

'I have been studying how I may compare
The prison where I live unto the world.'

William Shakespeare – Richard II

Isolation is the plughole to despair! When we withdraw from the world, shut others out, our world diminishes and becomes a prison.

It's so easy with supermarkets, TV and curtains to shut ourselves away, and think that we feel comfortable.

Maybe our withdrawal is not that extreme, but if we catch ourselves starting to shut the world out, we want to take countermeasures.

We can be surrounded by people and noise all the time and continually respond on autopilot. We camouflage our isolation in a crowd, never allowing ourselves to be honest with others.

'Where would I find the time?'

And yet to have sanity, balance, joy, fulfilment in our lives, we need to have regular, honest interaction with others. We want to talk honestly about what is going on inside, or it will fester.

'People tell me there are a lot of guys like me, which doesn't explain why I'm lonely.'

Mort Sahl

January 11

Attitudes

'The greatest discovery of my generation is that a human being can alter his life by altering his attitudes of mind.'

William James

Inactivity, disquiet, feeling disgruntled, frustrated or preoccupied are all potential stepping stones to doom. The more they creep into our lives, the more insidious they are. They arrive unannounced and unnoticed and consume us. It is like walking into a fog, there are a few wisps of cloud which we don't notice, then a few more and suddenly we're in thick fog. We don't know how we got there, and we have no idea how to get out.

To feel anything, anger, lethargy, happiness, we have to do it with our bodies before we can do it with our minds. So if we don't like how we feel, the first, and the vital thing to do, is to change our body. Get up, move around, do different things. We cannot feel happy if we shuffle along with our head down. We cannot feel depressed if we smile, put our shoulders back and march down the road. (If you don't believe that, do it and experience the difference.)

Once we've changed our body – and so our mind, we can decide on the actions to take and start the journey towards possibilities.

Interact with others positively. Make someone smile. If you don't feel like it, do it anyway, pretend.

Dare to dream and start taking the actions to achieve. Little things lead on to greater things.

'Nothing is settled, everything can still be altered.'

Claude Lévi-Strauss

January 12

Presence

'Regret for the things we did can be tempered by time; it is regret for the things we did not do that is inconsolable.'

Sydney J Harris

We talk about spending quality, not quantity time. But are we being honest? Do we give individual attention? Do we leave 'our business' outside and go in prepared to do 'whatever is needed.' And if we do start like that, can we sustain that selfless attitude throughout the time we spend doing what we set out to do.

It's keeping our eye on the ball throughout that's important. For as anyone who has ever hit a ball knows, if we take our eye off it, we miss, or miss-hit.

Arnold Schwarzenegger was Mr Universe for many years, he stated, "To lift a weight once with thought, is better than lifting it ten times without thought."

So if we are going to spend time, make sure it is quality time. Whether the quality is the way we undertake a task or the way we share ourselves with others.

Let's make sure the way we spend our time rewards everybody.

'If we did all the things, we were capable of, we would literally astound ourselves.'

Thomas Edison

January 13

Beauty

'Beauty will save the world.'

Fyodor Dostoevsky

Love and beauty walk hand in hand.

When we love, we notice beauty everywhere.

There is always beauty if we take but a moment to indulge in it.

Beauty and love walk hand in hand.

Whether we are in love or open to love, beauty exists. When we are out of love, beauty is still there.

If we find beauty, it can awaken love within us.

If we cultivate love, it turns on the lights, beauty increases, and so does our quality of life.

'Much love, much trial, but what an utter desert is life without love.'

Charles Darwin

January 14

Children

'Your children are not your children.... You are the bows from which your children as living arrows are sent forth.... You may give them your love but not your thoughts.... You may house their bodies but not their souls.'

Kahlil Gibran

It is so easy to be frustrated when they won't do... what we very reasonably... want them... expect them... to do.

It might help us, perhaps, if we were to cast our minds back to when we were children.

To remember our frustrations because our parents 'wouldn't' understand, in fact, 'couldn't' understand, and so there was no point in explaining anything to them.

It is also worth bearing in mind how 'charming', (if we're lucky), our children's friends may seem. And that's probably because neither they nor we are placing demands on each other.

It may also be that we are falling into the trap of 'Do as I say - Not what I do.' We learn from what we see people doing and not what they say.

"So give love, give space, give time and give more love."

Enjoy them while you can.

Do your best to be enjoyable for them.

'They fuck you up, your mum and dad.
They may not mean to, but they do.
They fill you with the faults they had.
And add some extra, just for you!'

Philip Larkin

January 15

Perfectionism

'Whoever thinks a faultless piece to see,
Thinks what ne'er was, nor is, nor e'er shall be.'

Alexander Pope

Some of us are cursed, to various degrees with perfectionism. [The most severely cursed may be blind to the fact that it is a curse.]

One of its disadvantages is that we set unreachable goals for ourselves and others, and so, everyone suffers.

Another common side-effect of perfectionism is that if there isn't time to do the job 'properly' it never gets started.

People who are the opposite, the 'let's give it a go and see what happens' people, achieve vastly more than the perfectionist ever will. Okay, 10% of what they may do fails, but 90% has some degree of success. And they've done all that before the perfectionist has even finished his breakfast!

So if you do suffer from the dreaded 'P' get out there and give it a go. It doesn't matter if it's not perfect. You can always tweak it later, or even abandon it. The world won't end.

Go on! Have some fun!

Definitely – if you don't want to!

'Well nobody's perfect.'

Osgood Fielding III (Billy Wilder) – Some Like It Hot

January 16

Attitude

'Start every day off with a smile and get it over with.'

W C Fields

'Gaiety is the most outstanding feature of the Soviet Union.'

Joseph Stalin

Some people take life too seriously!

They trudge through their day from one 'problem' to the next, never stopping to breathe the air or smell the flowers. They immerse themselves in the news, reading papers, focusing on all the troubles in the world, their lives, and the shortcomings of others.

If any of that 'just might' apply to you, reduce your intake of the news to once a day. Only watch the headlines. Don't read about the rapes and murders and the dreadful things that man does to man.

Challenge yourself to start identifying the 'good aspects' in people.

Become the bearer of good news, and bring light into the lives of everyone you know.

Decide to have fun. You're only here once.

'Not a shred of evidence exists in favour of the idea that life is serious.'

Brendan Gill

January 17

Judging

'How wise are thy commandments, Lord. Each of them applies to somebody I know.'

Sam Levenson

It's so easy to point the finger, to judge others. But when we point our finger at someone, three of our own fingers are pointing back at us.

But regardless of that 'clever' saying, when we judge others, we can be sure, if we can be honest enough to look at ourselves, that we are carrying a whole pile of our own shit around.

Personal housecleaning, recognition of our faults and shortcomings is a start. But it is not only our major wrongdoings that we should consider, they are easy to recognise, to confess and amend. It is the little, thoughtless daily acts that are inconsiderate towards others, that need constant work.

When our focus is on how to improve the lives of others, we can begin to live.

'There is sin in every single one of us and if we would fight evil, then let us fight the wrong within our own being.'

James Mawdsley

January 18

Self-forgetting

'For it is by self-forgetting that one finds.'

St Francis of Assisi

We live in a world where most people are striving to get ahead. Where many people are spiritually bankrupt, and even those who follow a religion, actually spend far more time and energy following material fulfilment.

They are searching for the next fix to satisfy themselves – which is why shopping and eating become compulsive.

We chase our tails to fill every moment, never achieving our needs because our needs have become unobtainable.

By self-forgetting, by taking the focus off ourselves, and achieving satisfaction by helping others, we can have peace of mind and tranquility, we can accomplish a wholeness that we have forgotten.

Then we will be truly satisfied.

'VLADIMIR: That passed the time.
ESTRAGON: It would have passed in any case.
VLADIMIR: Yes, but not so rapidly.'

Samuel Beckett

January 19

Lies

'She tells enough white lies to ice a wedding cake.'

Margot Asquith

'Not Guilty.'

O J Simpson

We all tell lies.

And however small they are, they damage us.

They roll off our tongue, without wiping their feet, with cherubic innocence, because it's easier. We've messed up before. We are not going to admit it this time.

It probably all stems from our mothers asking, 'Have you washed your hands?'

But whatever the reason, however unimportant our fibs may be, we know. And we punish ourselves because we know.

Even when we get away with it, although we may feel triumphant at the success, part of us feels ashamed. And the feeling of shame starts to isolate us from the world.

Shame lives in a dark place, where we do not want to go. Why would we choose to add to that with more dishonesty?

'We think caged birds sing, when indeed they cry.'

John Webster

January 20

Inventory

'When a stupid man is doing something he is ashamed of, he always declares that it is his duty.'

George Bernard Shaw

Are there things that we do that don't sit quite right with who we are, and if we were totally honest, make us feel slightly uncomfortable? Do we do things alone, that we wouldn't do if someone else were there?

When we are with others, do we only have one biscuit, while when on our own, we have six or finish the packet?

Do we rule our house with the 'Do as I say – Not what I do' adage? If we do, then what in the long run, do we imagine the outcome will be?

Look honestly at your behaviour and question yourself about it. You can then choose whether to change or accept it.

In the final analysis, we know what's right or wrong, and which we choose is up to us.

'I know of only one duty, and that is to love.'

Albert Camus

January 21

Attitude

'I am more and more convinced that our happiness or unhappiness depends far more on the way we meet the events of life, than on the nature of those events themselves.'

Wilhelm von Humboldt

Sometimes we do not feel as if we 'belong', we feel at odds with or alienated from the people in the world around us.

At times like this, it is good to remember that others are doing the best they can at this time. And so are we.

And so the emotions we feel, the highs, the lows, the separateness, are the same as the emotions they feel. We are all the same. We all belong to one another.

'The remarkable thing is, we have a choice every day regarding the attitude we will embrace for that day. We cannot change our past. We cannot change the fact that people will act in a certain way. We cannot change the inevitable. The only thing we can do is play the one string we have, and that is our attitude.'

Charles R Swindoll

January 22

Life

'We never do anything well till we cease to think about the manner of doing it.'

William Hazlitt

'It is not the things we accomplish that are important, it is the very act of living that is truly important.'

Dr Bill Jackson

It is all a game. Life is a game. People take everything so seriously – when it isn't.

In the grand scheme of things, what happens to us is no more important than what happens to a speck of dust floating a few million miles between the earth and the sun.

And yet everyone takes it all so seriously. If you and a friend played a game of tennis, for fun for an hour, you would both play your best, but after you'd finish, you'd walk away, and it would not be of any great consequence. In truth, nothing in our life is of any more importance than that game of tennis. When we look back over our life, everything will have washed away and spiraled down a plughole.

If we can realise this now, it frees us to get on with our lives, to move from one game to the next. Enjoying some more than others, but not concerned about the things that don't go the way we think they should.

'If a thing is worth doing, it is worth doing badly.'

G K Chesterton

'I can't see who's in the lead, but it's either Oxford or Cambridge.'

John Snagge (Commentating on the Boat Race.)

January 23

Positivity

'Refuse to be ill. Never tell people you are ill; never own it to yourself. Illness is one of those things a man should resist on principle.'

Edward Bulwer-Lytton

What we say may not appear significant, but unfortunately, our unconscious listens to everything.

Let's take the simple statement "I'm tired." Our unconscious hears this and eager to please says "Oh I can do that, I'm good at that" and makes us feel tired. If it's just before bed that's fine, but say it at breakfast, and we launch ourselves into a few hours or even a day of tiredness.

A pre-eminent question to ask oneself is, 'Is this what I want?' Do we want to feel tired, depressed, irritated, nagged, ill, a failure, pissed off, shy, unable to concentrate? If we do not want to experience those feelings – why say them?

Learn to say the positive, the good, the things we do want. I feel fit, healthy, enthusiastic, confident, etc.

Our unconscious listens to everything and does it's best to create in us what it sees and hears. So any negatives we hear, from ourselves, our family, friends, at work, in the bus queue, on TV, feed our unconscious. The news is probably the most significant source of negativity in our lives. Turn it off.

And remember "Is this what I want?" and if not, change what you're saying, listening to and watching.

'Oh heavens, how I long for a little ordinary human enthusiasm. Just enthusiasm – that's all. I want to hear a warm thrilling voice cry out Hallelujah! Hallelujah! I'm alive.'

John Osborne

January 24

Fulfilment

'I have met a great many people on their way towards God, and I wonder why they have chosen to look for him, rather than themselves.'

Jeanette Winterson

There is a story about a man who decided to leave his farm and go and search for diamonds. He had many adventures, extreme hardships, and towards the end of his life, was shipwrecked. He made his way ashore and found himself back on his farm, and as he lay dying in a field strewn with pebbles, he realised that they were diamonds.

Our peace, our light, our treasure lies within us. We can find it wherever and whenever we choose. We can stop searching and start accepting.

We are the light in our lives. We are the only light. Only we can access it and choose to let it out. We are as magnificent and complete as we allow ourselves to be.

'Know thyself.'

Greek, written in the temple at Delphi

'Our remedies oft in ourselves do lie,
Which we ascribe to heaven.'

William Shakespeare – All's Well That Ends Well

January 25

Learning

'But I'm such a bad scholar, I feel like a man with a white cane knocking into knowledge.'

Peter Carey

Our journey through life is as a student, hopefully, learning as we go.

We may not want all our lessons – and that's too bad. Many of our lessons come from experiences we may wish we hadn't had, and these are often the most important.

Our journey through life is as a teacher, and to be able to teach and give, we have to learn.

We never know it all. To stop learning is to cut oneself off from the world. As we teach, we learn, for lessons change with every telling.

The trick to it all is willingness, openness and humility, and an honest desire to give and to receive.

'A teacher affects eternity; he can never tell where his influence stops.'

Henry Brooks Adams

'There is no such whetstone, to sharpen a good wit and encourage a will to learning, as is praise.'

Roger Ascham

January 26

Detachment

'Always remember that you were once alone, and the crowd you see in your life today are just as unnecessary as when you were alone.'

Michael Bassey Johnson

Sometimes – just sometimes you understand – sometimes living with someone else can be... stressful, even when they are well-meaning.

And engaging with them... it can be a... struggle... even a challenge.

Especially when we're in there, down, and dirty, full of emotion.

YEAH!

An alternative way of being is to move out of your body and watch the scene as it unfolds. Watch you and them from a corner of the room. When we do this, because we are not in our bodies, we do not get emotionally involved.

We and the others do our bit, however, because we are now detached, everything is so much easier.

(Experiment with it, do it, move out of your body and watch yourself in stress-free situations, and then when difficulties appear, you will know how to do it.)

Don't forget to go back into your body when you want to do things that you enjoy.

'Hope not, despair not... the human race is the human race. Nothing can be done about it.'

Marty Rubin

January 27

Living

'Seize the moment. Remember all those women on the Titanic who waved off the dessert cart.'

Erma Bombeck

So often we put things off, and then we never do them.

'Let's go to the seaside'

'Tomorrow maybe' or 'Do you think the weather's good enough?' or 'We're already too late, think of the traffic.' Or 'Oh, I was planning to mow the lawn.' Or 'The football's on.' Or 'Can we afford it?'

Maybe you've never had that conversation, but most people do not do things on impulse. It just doesn't fit in with their way of life. The excuses they come up with really have nothing to do with the event, and they are knee jerk reactions to the unexpected.

Take risks!

It doesn't matter if it isn't perfect.

Live!

Have adventures.

Fill your life with moments to look back on with relish.

Enjoy the disasters and successes.

Do it anyway!

'Life is not always a matter of holding good cards, but sometimes of playing a poor hand well.'

Robert Louis Stevenson

'Life is too short to be small.'

Benjamin Disraeli

January 28

Amends

'I am a man
More sinned against than sinning.'

William Shakespeare. King Lear

So many of us go through life thinking, 'he did it to me', or 'I'm not going to apologise, it was their fault'. We absolutely know that they started it, if anything is going to change, they will have to apologise, we're not going to forgive them.

And so we crawl along with a collection of black clouds, that keep the sunshine out of our lives.

For our peace of mind, for a trouble-free journey through life, we want to apologise. Even if we know, it is not our fault. And more often than not, halfway through our apology, they will be claiming that they were at fault.

Whether they accept any responsibility or not, we want to make amends for any of the wrongs we have done, and to apologise face to face if that is possible. (We almost certainly don't want to do it face to face, but we know that this is how it wants to be done.)

'I only ask to be free. The butterflies are free.'

Charles Dickens

January 29

Self-love

'Wherever you go, go with all your heart.'

Confucius

If you only had this week, seven days, to do something, anything you like, and after that – nothing – what would you choose? What would you do?

This requires reflection, then a decision and finally, action.

Most of us spend our lives like flies around a cowpat, bobbing up and down, landing, leaving, going nowhere.

And yet we know we're only here once. We know it's going to end. Surely that would encourage even the dimmest person to do something meaningful.

Wherever we are, however restricted our life, if nothing else, we can affect our attitude to our last seven days.

Do you have a list of a hundred things to do before you die? Or ten, or even one thing?

If you met someone who had a list and was doing the things on it, how would you feel? Would it inspire you? Or would you just creep away like a kicked puppy?

'After seeing "Rambo" last night I know what to do the next time this happens.'

Ronald Reagan

'To say yes, you have to sweat and roll up your sleeves and plunge both hands into life up to the elbows.'

Jean Anouilh

'If you add only a little to a little and do this often, soon that will become great.'

Hesiod

January 30

Lies

'We tell lies when we are afraid... afraid of what we don't know, afraid of what others will think, afraid of what will be found out about us. But every time we tell a lie, the thing that we fear grows stronger.'

Tad Williams

We lie to those close to us, to protect them (we think) from the things that are troubling our minds.

'What could they do?' we ask ourselves, 'It would only worry them. I can, and I must handle this alone.'

And maybe they cannot do anything to help us, except to say 'We're here for you. It will all work out in the end.'

If it does worry them, they love us, and they would prefer to be frightened by our words, than by our silence.

Our silence, our refusal to talk, is a scary and impenetrable place for them, it is worse than the truth.

Secrets that we keep to ourselves have the habit of growing stronger and darker and more unmanageable.

When we have troubles, let's open the door and let them out.

'The cruelest lies are often told in silence.'

Robert Louis Stevenson

January 31

Thoughts

'My thought is me: that is why I can't stop. I exist because I think... and I can't stop myself from thinking.'

Jean-Paul Sartre

We may think this is true, but it is not, of course. Our minds fill us with the chatter and insane babble of the past and the future, constantly distracting us from this moment, from what is actually happening.

I used to listen to people saying things like 'This moment is all we have' and 'We've only got the now' and think 'Yeah sure', but I didn't believe or understand. They'd say things like 'Yesterday's gone, tomorrow is promised to no one', and I would nod. I was ignorant. But now I believe, and I do understand. It is very liberating.

Meditation can teach us to go into the stillness of this moment.

When we go into this moment, we discover peace, the chatter falls away, vanishes and we can begin to know clearly who and why we are.

We can experience joy and freedom.

'The trouble with most people is that they think with their hopes or fears or wishes rather than with their minds.'

Will Durant

'Silence is as deep as Eternity; speech is shallow as Time.'

Thomas Carlyle

Enjoy

February 1

Arrogance

'There's nothing like eavesdropping to show you that the world outside your head is different from the world inside your head.'

Thornton Wilder

I know who I am.

~~~

I know what's right.

~~~

I know what's wrong.

~~~

I wear blinkers!

~~~

It's so easy to never stop and see oneself from over there. To believe that people see us as we imagine they do. To never question what their opinion might be. And if it does cross our minds that in some way, they look down on us, we take it with a pinch of salt.

And so, we march through our lives, sticking to the road we have created. Like royalty, waving graciously to the crowds as we pass.

Maybe, just maybe, our lives would be better if we were to dismount, long enough to explore what others think of us, to look at ourselves, and then choose who and how we would really like to be.

'It is much more difficult to judge oneself than to judge others.'

Antoine de Saint-Exupéry

February 2

Fun

'When I'm good I'm very good, but when I'm bad I'm better.'

Mae West

Sometimes we keep ourselves on too tight a rein, always denying ourselves things.

Then we break our rules mindlessly and feel bad about what we've done.

Far better to make a conscious decision to be reckless, to go out and do things, to have fun, to involve others in our extravagance. And so to have a joyous memory to look back on.

It also makes further periods of 'being good' easier to accept, because we can look forward to another adventure in the joy of living.

Don't lead a dull life.

All work and no play makes Jack a dull boy!

Have fun.

'Hatcheck girl: "Goodness, what beautiful diamonds!"
Mae West: "Goodness had nothing to do with it, dearie!" '

Mae West

February 3

Self Esteem

'The reason we struggle with insecurity is because we compare our behind-the-scenes with everyone else's highlight reel.'

Steve Furtick

From the moment we start our lives, we are pitched into competition with everyone about us, compared to our siblings, contemporaries, parents, grandparents, in fact, the world.

It starts with them "doing it to us" but in no time at all, even if we have mastered little else, we have mastered the ability to see if we measure up.

And nobody measures up everywhere, not even the most successful of us. We do not have to be better than them, or even as good as they are.

There is always room for insecurity, and it is easy to find some way of shooting ourselves in the foot.

We want to accept ourselves and enjoy what we do.

Doing things well, because that is what we choose to do – not because we need to prove anything. Doing things badly because that is what we choose to do – not because we want to get our own back. Or just being average because we are – and that's okay.

We are who we are, so we might as well feel good about ourselves. (Pass the doughnuts.)

'What other dungeon is so dark as one's own heart! What jailor so inexorable as one's self!'

Nathaniel Hawthorne

February 4

Travel

'Unanticipated invitations to travel are dancing lessons from God.'

Kurt Vonnegut

How comfortable it is to sit at home and watch travel programs on TV.

How easy it is to do the same thing as last year – because it is okay and it's what we know.

If only we were to open our diary now and choose a time, not far away, to have an adventure, to do something completely new.

A weekend break in Moscow, Cairo, or Marrakesh.

A week whale watching, seeing the Northern Lights, scuba diving, skiing, exploring Brazil, taking a walking holiday, to go boating, working on a ranch.

You choose. We're only here once. Don't die on 'Someday Isle' – 'Someday I'll go to Australia' – 'Someday I'll do something new.'

Of course, there are excuses, 'Reasons', there always are, but when did that ever stop us from doing what we really wanted to do.

'A sure cure for seasickness is to sit up a tree.'

Spike Milligan

February 5

Anxiety

'But what torments of grief you endured
From evils which never arrived.'

Ralph Waldo Emerson

That knot in the stomach. The feeling that we may be sick before we... make our appearance. It may be a huge event or just a little one, but it is enormous to us, and we find ourselves crippled with anxiety.

Some famous actors have thrown up every night of their lives before going on stage, to a rapturous reception.

What is happening is that our body is filling us with adrenalin, so that we can fight the predator or run like mad to get away from it. The adrenalin is there so that we can perform brilliantly. Unfortunately, most of us don't know this, we feel the hit of adrenalin and think 'Oh my God, I feel sick with fear.' Rather than thinking 'I feel like this because my body is giving me everything I need to go out there and do the most fabulous job.'

So now, all we have to do is to decide which reaction we'd rather have when we get the feeling and start having it.

'O! that man might know
The end of this days business ere it come.'

William Shakespeare – Julius Caesar

February 6

Meditation

'I think a spiritual journey is not so much a journey of discovery. It's a journey of recovery. It's a journey of uncovering your own inner nature. It's already there.'

Billy Corgan

I used to think that to meditate you had to live in Tibet for 30 years, eating boiled rice, (and I don't like boiled rice.)

I discovered that this wasn't necessary. Meditation is easy to do, and it doesn't need to take more than a few minutes once a day, to make an incredible difference to your life. However, if you can do it 2 or 3 times a day, even better.

When I meditate the coincidences happen, I'm in the right place, at the right time.

This is what I do. Before I start, I tell myself what I want to achieve, to feel. These things can be short or long term. Then I close my eyes, count from 10-1, relax my body, go inside, feel my inner energy, and concentrate on my breathing. I then repeat the instructions I gave myself before I started. In due course, I count 1-10 and come back out.

There are thousands of different ways to meditate, explore some. There are apps that you can use. Find what suits you. Do it for a few minutes a day. Transform your life.

'Happiness is not achieved by the conscious pursuit of happiness; it is generally the by-product of other activities.'

Aldous Huxley

February 7

Truth

'Truth, like time, is an idea arising from, and dependent upon, human intercourse. What is the truth about a mountain in Africa that has no name and not even a footpath across it?'

Isak Dinesen

It is so easy to believe that we know the right way to do things and to think that our beliefs are the truth.

It is often difficult to contemplate that this might not be so.

Suppose we can learn to keep an open mind. If we can allow ourselves and others, the freedom to experiment, with new ways of thinking and doing things, we would lead far more fulfilling lives.

If we lived in a box, and that was all we knew, it would be our world and our reality. It would be unthinkable that anyone could open up a part of it and let in the light and...

'Let a man get up and say, "Behold, this is the truth", and instantly I perceive a sandy cat filching a piece of fish in the background. Look, you have forgotten the cat, I say.'

Virginia Woolf

February 8

Acceptance

'Reality is what I see, not what you see.'

Woodrow Wilson

Life happens, and we react.

If we see someone have an accident, it immediately creates a feeling within us. We do what we can to help (or not), but we don't blame the victim for making us feel the way we do.

And yet as we go through our day, and feel, good – bad, happy – sad, angry – loving, it's easy to imagine that our feelings come from what is happening around us or to us, or from what we are doing.

We point our finger at the apparent cause of our emotions. We blame 'the events' and allow any negative emotions we may have to fester and poison us. However, we are creating our feelings ourselves.

It is such a relief, such a breath of fresh air when we stop doing this and learn to exercise our right to choose how we feel.

Nobody else can make us feel things. We do it to ourselves.

'There is something that can be found in one place. It is a great treasure which may be called the fulfilment of existence. The place where this treasure can be found is the place where one stands.'

Martin Buber

February 9

Tolerance

'If a madman were to come into this room with a stick in his hand, no doubt we would pity his state of mind; but our primary consideration would be to take care of ourselves. We should knock him down first, and pity him afterwards.'

Samuel Johnson

We read that from the viewpoint of the sane man. But what if we were the madman?

And haven't we all at some moment in our lives been the madman? 'No! No!' We cry! 'Not me!'

But have we never done anything that afterwards we felt was, perhaps, 'Not the best thing we could have done?'

And if so, why did we do it?

Here's an explanation:- Given the situation that we are in, and the person we are, we all do the best we can at that moment in time.

Let's repeat that – Given the situation that we are in, and the person we are, we all do the best we can at that moment in time. And sometimes, the best we could do at that moment was truly awful. But it was still the best we could do – at that moment.

So, we want to realise that we're not perfect and what matters is how we choose to act the next.

We also want to remember that others are also doing the best they can. And if we find that unbearable, then we need to make changes to the situation that we are in with them, so that their behaviour can change.

If nothing changes, then nothing will change.

'This creature is very wicked. He defends himself when attacked.'

Théodore P K

February 10

Time

'Half our life is spent trying to find something to do with the time we have rushed through life trying to save.'

Will Rogers

And so we waste the time we've saved, and yet at the same time often say, 'I don't have time to... '

We bounce through our lives like a ball in a pinball machine, knocked this way and that by flippers, pushed by someone else.

Preoccupied with 'really important' things, we don't notice what could be truly meaningful in our lives if we were to give it our attention.

Occasionally there are moments when the mist of preoccupation clears and we have a chance to take stock, to be proactive, to decide to take notice of and do the things that matter.

But blink... You've missed it.

Grab it and fill your life with meaning and joy.

'She did not recognise her enemy,
She thought him dust:
But what is dust,
Save time's most lethal weapon,
His faithful ally and our sneaking foe.'

Osbert Sitwell

February 11

Choice

'Boredom is the root of all evil.'

Søren Kierkegaard

Sometimes we slip into a state of mind when life appears stale.

The repetitiveness of it all becomes too tedious.

Which of the same old boring things shall we do, to kill time until...

True, it's often not as bad, or as obvious as that. Sometimes it's just a little mental tap on the shoulder, a sigh, a wisp of resignation that creeps into our lives.

But, if all we have is now, why would we choose to feel like that? Surely, we want to be rejoicing in the moment. So, don't let the 'I'm bored' flutter into our mind, don't go down the 'What have I got to do now?' road.

Instead think, with anticipation 'What shall I do next?'

And when you've chosen, decide that it is what you want to do.

Decide to enjoy it.

It's more fun that way.

'The cure for boredom is curiosity. There is no cure for curiosity.'

Dorothy Parker

February 12

Forgiveness

'Once a woman has forgiven her man, she must not reheat his sins for breakfast.'

Marlene Dietrich

Although we may be as pure as falling snow, we've all done things that need forgiving.

We also, and sometimes this is even harder, need to forgive ourselves.

Failure to forgive others or ourselves creates an enormous burden for us to carry, and we may stumble under its weight.

The Lord's Prayer requests 'Forgive us our trespasses, As we forgive those who trespass against us.' The critical word there is 'As'. If we cannot or do not forgive others, we cannot and will not be able to forgive ourselves.

We may need help, prayer, sharing, to be able to forgive. The benefits of genuinely forgiving ourselves and others are immeasurable.

'I can forgive, but I cannot forget, is only another way of saying, I will not forgive. Forgiveness ought to be like a cancelled note, torn in two, and burned up, so that it never can be shown against one.'

Henry Ward Beecher

February 13

Blame

'Well if I called the wrong number, why did you answer the phone?'

James Thurber

Sometimes we're so quick to blame. 'It's your fault!' 'How can he /she/you be so... '

And when we accuse anyone, it should be like the bell that they ring at "Lloyds of London Insurers" when a ship sinks. It's a wakeup call, telling us that there is something wrong – with us.

What is even worse is when we blame ourselves for everything and feel worthless, because we can then torture ourselves with it for an age. It is rare for everything to be our fault, there are nearly always others involved, who bear some of the responsibility for what has happened.

Self-blame and self-loathing do not make anything better, any more than guilt does. When something has gone wrong, we want to work out what we can do next, not rant, shout, or shrivel up inside, because of what has happened.

There are times when we blame others for not recognising or crediting us enough for what we've done. We want to learn to be able to be proud of ourselves without needing outside recognition. Recognition is great, but not essential.

'God said to Abraham, "Kill me a son."
Abe says "Man you must be putting me on"'

Bob Dylan

February 14

Ego

'Faith takes the sting from adversity,
And provides a calming peace in stormy waters.'

Michael Ganly

Peace is only possible in the present. It is only possible when we let go of the future and all the unknown boulders that might lie ahead. We also have to discard the past and all the troubles that we've accumulated.

As long as we travel backwards and, or forwards, we cannot experience peace.

By letting go, by becoming at one with our body and the present, we can enjoy genuine peace.

A voice in our heads, rabbits on, endlessly telling us what to worry about and how to think.

Stop listening to it. Just observe the words it babbles, and realise that they are not real. They are not your friend. They are just the ego's / the mind's way of preventing us from having peace.

By letting go, relaxing, observing, it's possible to have peace.

Listen for and hear the still, calm voice that waits quietly behind the noise. Discover that you can do and achieve things that you may have thought impossible.

Feel the inner smile.

'What is peace? Is it war? No. Is it strife? No. Is it lovely, and gentle, and beautiful, and pleasant, and serene, and joyful? O yes!'

Charles Dickens

February 15

Responsibility

'It matters not how strait the gate,
How charged with punishments the scroll,
I am the master of my fate:
I am the captain of my soul.'

W E Henley

How wonderful to discover that we are responsible for ourselves and that everyone else is responsible for themselves, this means that we are <u>not</u> responsible for 'them'. We may want to think we are, but we are not.

We can choose to do all we can for them, but in the end, they are responsible for themselves.

I can do all I can to teach my son how to cross the road, but if he chooses to run in front of a car, he is responsible.

We cannot live their lives for them.

Accepting this gives us freedom. It also liberates others, and then they can grow. And it may even give us the ability to help them in ways that we cannot if we believe that we are responsible.

'The finest gift you can give anyone is encouragement. Yet, almost no one gets the encouragement they need to grow to their full potential. If everyone received the encouragement they need to grow, the genius in most everyone would blossom, and the world would produce abundance beyond our wildest dreams.'

Sidney Madwed

February 16

Depression

'You may not know it, but at the far end of despair, there is a white clearing where one is almost happy.'

Joan Baez

We all have times when we travel through dark periods. Moments which feel endless and without hope.

When we are in them, we draw them ever closer around us, like a duvet, hiding in their darkness, absorbed in ourselves.

When we are not in them, we cannot actually remember them. We forget the blackness, and our unconscious will not let us relive the total experience, lest we explode.

If we raise our chin off the floor and look around us, look for someone, anyone, whom we can help, our lot will improve.

Taking our eyes off ourselves disempowers our despair.

And it is vital to remember that in just the same way that good times pass, our bad times will too.

It is also important to remember that we all have ups and downs. We are human, and we can choose where we focus our minds.

'Despair is the greatest of our errors.'

Luc de Clapiers

'The Devil, having nothing else to do,
Went off to tempt My Lady Poltagrue.
My Lady, tempted by a private whim,
To his extreme annoyance, tempted him.'

Hilaire Belloc

February 17

Action

'We act as though comfort and luxury were the chief requirements of life, when all we need to make us really happy is something to be enthusiastic about.'

Charles Kingsley

Luxury and comfort differ vastly from person to person, and the same is right about enthusiasm. If we are not looking forward to anything, we want to wonder why?

The thing(s) that we choose to look forward to can be tiny if that is where our horizon is. But once we have chosen something to look forward to, be enthusiastic about, we can start to enjoy the journey.

The object of our enthusiasm may do absolutely nothing for the people in our lives. But if they are not supportive, it does not mean that we should give up. If everybody gave up as soon as someone questioned what they wanted to achieve, nobody would ever do anything.

It is probably sensible though not to follow our dream with total disregard to others.

And if our goal is not making us happy, maybe we want to reassess what we're doing, where we are going and why.

'Three grand essentials to happiness in this life are something to do, something to love, and something to hope for.'

Joseph Addison

February 18

Imagination

'Imagination is more important than knowledge. For knowledge is limited whereas imagination embraces the entire world.'

Albert Einstein

We all imagine things. Imagining successful outcomes in our lives increases the likelihood that they will materialise.

A group of students who spent an hour a day visualising themselves shooting successful basketball hoops increased their success rate more than another group who spent an hour a day in the gym actually shooting hoops.

To take the time – even a little time – visualising success in what we are about to do, makes an incredible difference.

We need to beware, not everybody will want us to succeed, and if they throw in seeds of failure, our unconscious can plant them and create expectations of failure in us. We don't want to allow our imagination to feed us pictures of failure.

The more details we can visualise, the more successful pictures we create, the bigger the emotions and positive feelings we add, the greater our chance of success.

'To see a World in a Grain of Sand,
And a Heaven in a Wild Flower,
Hold infinity in the palm of your hand,
And Eternity in an hour.'

William Blake

February 19

Habits

'Have you ever noticed that anybody driving slower than you is an idiot, and anyone going faster than you is a maniac.'

George Carlin

We're so in the habit of jumping in our car to nip off and... It's almost as if we had forgotten that we have legs, or that there is any other form of transport.

At the risk of appearing to change the subject – most of us find it challenging to remember to do mini-meditations throughout the day. One way to remind ourselves is to anchor meditation to any action we often do, it can be anything, like having a pee. If you get in and out of your car regularly, make a habit of closing your eyes for a minute, taking a deep breath and meditating.

We may feel free driving, but in fact, it limits us. and our ability to take in and enjoy the world. (Try being a passenger and see how much more you experience.)

Our car isolates us from the world, keeping us in another little cage. Let's find ways to use it less and participate more.

'Why do they call it rush hour when nothing moves?'

Robin Williams

'Take it easy driving – the life you save may be mine.'

James Dean

'Beneath this slab
John Brown is stowed.
He watched the ads,
And not the road.'

Ogden Nash

February 20

Freedom

'Never forget that only dead fish swim with the stream.'

Malcolm Muggeridge

'Whoso would be a man, must be a nonconformist.'

Ralph Waldo Emerson

How easy it is to conform. From the year dot, we have conformity drummed into us. We may have had a teenage/early twenties rebellion, but most of us, even then, are only conforming with the rest of our peer group.

To be different, to be oneself, to be unique is difficult. It takes great courage not to do things the way other people do them.

We nearly all have brief moments when we dare to do things differently, to let our hair down. When we dare to choose who we want to be, what we want to do, and carry it out, it is terrific.

Become aware of which way the herd is walking and choose the opposite direction. Experiment. Get out of the comfort zone and relish the delight of

If you don't know where to start, take a risk, change things in your life and see what happens. The worst that can happen is that you just go back to the same old.

'If a man does not keep pace with his companions, perhaps it is because he hears a different drummer. Let him step to the music which he hears, however measured or far away.'

Henry David Thoreau

'Between two evils, I always pick the one I've never tried before.'

Mae West

February 21

Suffering

'A man will renounce any pleasures you like, but he will not give up his suffering.'

G I Gurdjieff

Why do they have to suffer? What is it that makes people cling onto their suffering, like a comfort blanket?

And how desperately impotent we can feel in our inability to help them.

Of course, our concern for them is a distraction from our suffering.

We suffer because we are consumed with either what has happened, or by what we perceive may happen. 50% of the things that happen, we have no control over, so there's no point in worrying about them. And the other 50% of things, are in our control, and so it is pointless to worry about them either.

We can only do one thing at any given time. By focusing totally on what we are doing now, and giving it our full attention, we can do it properly. We can then move onto the next thing. When we try to do/think about lots of things at once, we simply create suffering for ourselves.

So by being in this moment fully, not dwelling on the past, or losing ourselves in the future, we can be present now, and no longer suffer.

If we choose to, we can have peace. And if we decide to have peace now, we will be better equipped to deal with the future, if it arrives.

'Once this has happened, the last thing they want is to become free of them; that would mean loss of self. There can be a great deal of unconscious ego investment in pain and suffering.'

Eckhart Tolle

February 22

Memory

'God gave us memory so that we might enjoy roses in December.'

J M Barrie

Life changes. When people, places or things move out of our lives, we often remember them with sorrow – overwhelmed by what we miss.

We can remember wonderful times and fall into the 'Oh God, I'll never be able to do that again' trap. Or just go into the emptiness and all-consuming sorrow that the memory creates.

We do have a choice though, both about what we remember and how we choose to remember it. Instead of indulging in sorrow and blackness, we can start to think of the past with joy.

Relive the happiness, the joy, the delight.

The past is gone, all we have is this moment, being unhappy or happy about the past won't bring it back or change it. We can, however, choose to feel content now and enjoy our memories.

'As a perfume doth remain
In the folds where it hath lain,
So the thought of you remaining
Deeply folded in my brain,
Will not leave me: all things leave me:
You remain.'

Arthur Symons

February 23

Freedom

'Yes, 'n' how many years can some people exist
Before they're allowed to be free?
Yes, 'n' how many times can a man turn his head,
Pretending he just doesn't see?
The answer, my friend, is blowing in the wind.
The answer is blowing in the wind.'

Bob Dylan

Only we can give ourselves freedom.

Our life stands before us with promise. That we are here means that we have the strengths and power to live through it. Whatever confronts us, we will find a way to deal with the challenges.

The world may bear down on us, and remove our options, force us into having to live in ways that we might not like or want, but the world cannot control our thoughts.

We always have the freedom to think about what we want, and if we choose to feel empowered, however bad our lot, then we are free.

'They took away my freedom, not my liberty.'

Brian Keenan (a hostage in Lebanon)

February 24

Prayer

'Pray as if everything depended on God, work as if everything depended on man.'

Cardinal Spellman

Even if we are not the 'praying sort' most of us do pray at times of genuine stress. 'Get me out of here God... and I promise I will never... again... Honestly... I won't... '

And most of us would admit that this is not a meaningful prayer.

We want to regularly communicate with a higher power (let's call it God, it's a useful three-letter word). Just praying for ourselves doesn't work. We want to pray for the 'good for all concerned' without putting limits, specific demands, plans or pleas into our prayers.

It may be that what is 'good for all concerned' will not be the outcome that you would choose, but perhaps that outcome is the 'right' one, in the grand scheme of things, something that is beyond your comprehension.

To just say our prayers and wait for them to happen doesn't work either.

Prayer is action. So together with the prayer, we want to do whatever we can, to help the events to move towards achieving the 'good for all concerned'. We also want to thank God for enabling us to take the required action.

'In prayer it is better to have a heart without words than words without a heart.'

Mahatma Gandhi

February 25

Heaven

'Abandon hope all ye who enter here.'

Dante Alighieri

At my darkest hour, this is the only joke I found funny.

A man goes to heaven and finds three identical doors. St Peter says, 'You can choose whichever door you like.'

The man goes to each door and listens, through the first door, he can make out the sounds of nature. The middle door has a strange warbling sound coming from it. The last one has the unmistakable sounds of partying.

While he loves both nature and partying, his curiosity gets the better of him. He chooses the middle door.

He steps through, it slams behind him. He's standing on a very narrow ledge and in front of him is an enormous sea of shit. In the distance, a man standing on tiptoe, just his mouth and nose poking out. He's crying out, 'Don't make a wave... Don't make a wave... Don't make a wave...'

I found it funny because I was both the man shouting and the man on the shelf. When I've told this to people, the only ones who find it funny are the ones who have really suffered.

I tell it to you now, so that you can either laugh because you are moving to a better place, or simply be glad that you've never been there.

'I don't believe in heaven or hell, they're here; you choose which one you're going to be a lodger in.'

Tony Parker

'If a man could pass through Paradise in a dream, and have a flower presented to him as a pledge that his soul had really been there, and if he found that flower in his hand when he awoke – Aye, and what then?'

Samuel Taylor Coleridge

February 26

Choice

'Is that a pistol in your pocket or are you just pleased to see me?'

Mae West

Maybe it was a banana?

If we want to have control over what we eat, we need to have fruit with us.

Just suppose as you're walking along, you think that a doughnut or a bar of chocolate or a packet of biscuits would be yummy. There you are lost in the thought of the doughnut. What can you do? It's either a doughnut or a "nothing." Not much of a dilemma. The doughnut wins, even if you have to walk back 100 yards to get it.

However! If you have an apple with you, then you have an alternative. You may think that an apple is a poor substitute for a doughnut... but it does give you a choice. It's head and shoulders better than 'nothing', and if you do want to eat less, it's also head and shoulders above a doughnut.

So, stock up with fruit. Carry it with you. Reward yourself with it. Enjoy.

'An apple is an excellent thing – until you have tried a peach.'

George de Maurier

February 27

Gratitude

'When I look back on all these worries I remember the story of the old man who said on his deathbed that he had had a lot of troubles in his life, most of which had never happened.'

Winston Churchill

So easy to dwell on the difficulties of one's life. And even if one doesn't do that, it's easy not to appreciate all the good things in our lives.

If we make a list, a written list of the things in our lives that we are grateful for, it is a sparkling gem to carry forward, should we ever have moments when we struggle.

Only 10% (if that) of the people who read this will write a list – go on, surprise yourself, be one of the people who write it. Then every day choose only 1, 2 or 3 things that you are grateful for and go into your body and feel the gratitude. Feel it. Make it bigger. Let the feeling of joy and gratitude explode throughout you.

(Even if you don't make a list, please choose one thing today, and revel in your gratitude for it.)

It will make such a difference to your quality of life.

Go on, do yourself a favour, surprise yourself, be different, be filled with joy and gratitude and let the Brilliant White Light of Love fill you and shine out of you.

'Our memories are card-indexes consulted and then returned in disorder by authorities whom we do not control.'

Cyril Connolly

February 28

Experience

'Star light, star bright,
First star I see tonight,
I wish may, I wish might
Have the wish, I wish tonight.'

Anon

If we can rejoice when we see the evening star, the new moon, the full moon, the first glimpse of the sea as we drive towards it, the first daffodil. If we can rejoice, these moments are so so beautiful.

With the hum and the drum of our daily lives, it is so easy to forget to appreciate things, let alone to rejoice. It is so much easier to find fault and criticise.

Everything changes, all the time, we are not the person we were yesterday, nor the person we will be tomorrow. Every experience, however mundane, adds another stitch to the tapestry of our life.

Regardless of however many times we have done or experienced something, this time, now, is the first time we have experienced this event. We will never be able to repeat or undo this event and how we handle it.

If we choose to allow ourselves to rejoice in, experience this new event, it will be unique. Whatever we do, it will never happen again.

It is incredible to have a life filled with special moments.

'Some people are always grumbling because roses have thorns. I am thankful that thorns have roses.'

Alphonse Karr

'Life's a shit sandwich, be thankful for the bread.'

Random Homeless Guy

February 29

Happiness

'When you're smiling, When you're smiling,
The whole world smiles with you,'

Joe Goodwin

Smile at people. Keep doing it. Do and say things to get others to smile.

Chat to people in queues.

Ask people questions.

Say things that get them to look on the lighter side of life.

Don't be drawn into discussing the negative stuff with them.

So many people stumble through their days radiating glum.

Don't succumb.

Smile or better yet, laugh.

'When you're laughing, When you're laughing,
The sun comes shining through,'

Joe Goodwin

'She gave me a smile I could feel in my hip pocket.'

Raymond Chandler

Read...

Enjoy...

Share

March 1

Language

'My ambition has been so great it has never seemed to me worthwhile to try to satisfy it.'

Colonel Edward M House

'Trying is the first step to failure.'

Homer Simpson

I'm trying to! I'm trying to do this!

I'm trying to give that up. I'm really trying!

Will you do something with me now? Please put your hand on your knee. Now lift your hand up, then put it down. – You took action. Now try to lift it up. No! Don't lift it up. Try to lift it up. Trying is not lifting. Trying is not action.

Trying is a message to our unconscious to fail. Think of the times when someone says, 'I'll try and come for a coffee', and they don't. Think of the times you say you'll 'Try and do something,' and you don't. If you were honest with yourself, you know you're not going to do it when you say you'll try You just don't dare to tell them.

We want to banish the word try from our language. We want to have the courage of our convictions and say, 'Yes I'll do that.' or 'No, I won't do that'. Then they won't have to sit waiting for you for an hour. And we don't have to feel guilty about letting them down.

And it's the same with yourself, don't try to do something, decide you will, or you won't and carry it out.

If we say we are going to do something, we go for it, if we fail, we have feedback that we can use the next time we decide to do it, when hopefully we will succeed.

'When you change the way you look at things, the things you look at change.'

Wayne Dyer

March 2

Self-acceptance

'She had a blue skin, and so did he.
He kept it hid and so did she.
They searched for blue their whole life through,
Then passed right by – and never knew.'

Shel Silverstein

As we grow up, we create a shell around ourselves, which by and large we dare not peel back in public. Lest people were to realise... Lest they could see... us, in our true awfulness.

Maybe for you, that's an exaggeration. Perhaps you have no inner being that you are hiding. If so, that's wonderful. However, most of us have a façade that conceals us, it hides our secrets, but it also hides our light.

You don't need to dash around emotionally exposing yourself to all and sundry. Accept that you have a shell, as does everybody else.

If you can acknowledge that they are not who they present themselves to be either, you can be more accepting, less judgmental and more empathetic with them.

You can dare to start admitting to them that you exist – warts and all – and discover that they will, in turn, allow friendships where none existed before.

'Humankind must at last grow up. We must recognise that the other is ourselves.'

E P Thompson

March 3

Meditation

'Alas! I have no hope nor health,
Nor peace within nor calm around,
Nor that content surpassing wealth
The sage in meditation found.'

P B Shelley

Meditation is like insurance. It is no good going to the insurance company after your house has burnt down, wanting to take out insurance.

If we do not meditate when things are good, when we have peace of mind and happiness, then when things are less good, we will find that we cannot meditate. We have lost the ability to still the mind.

If we pay our premiums, by meditating regularly, then if faced with challenges, however black, we will still be able to meditate. We will be able to summon strength and energy, which will enable us to deal with problems and to rise from the ashes of disaster.

'I am told it works even if you don't believe in it'

Niels Bohr

'A believer is a songless bird in a cage, a freethinker is an eagle parting the clouds with tireless wing.'

R G Ingersoll

March 4

Weather

'Wherever you go, the weather is, without exception, exceptional.'

Kingsley Amis

It was a beautiful sunny day, I was walking down the hill in a foul mood, and I remember hating the weather. A couple of weeks later I was walking down the same hill, it was cold and raining, but I was in a fantastic mood, and I remember thinking how beautiful the day was.

And I realised at that moment, that I choose whether the weather is good, and if the day is good or not.

So I decided to have good days and good weather because I like them more. Since then, I have only had good weather. Sometimes I meet people who say, "Hasn't it been an awful summer?" and I look at them with shock, "No," I say, "it's been wonderful."

And I am not just saying that by rote, I am saying that because that is what I have experienced. I don't process lousy weather or bad days, so I don't recall them.

'This is the weather the cuckoo likes, and so do I.'

Thomas Hardy

March 5

Change

'Peel me a grape.'

Mae West

So you have a bunch of grapes. Do you eat the good ones first, or the bad ones first?

If we eat the bad ones first, then we are always eating bad grapes.

If we eat the good ones first, we never eat bad grapes, because, by the time we get to the bad ones, they have to be thrown away.

On consideration, if we do eat bad grapes first – we might choose to change our choice, not only for grapes but also for life.

However, the reason for mentioning any of this, is that if it applies to you, it means that you have rules about how to do things, and you enforce those same rules on others. For example, if you always eat the bad grapes, then to sit with someone who eats all the good grapes first, it would distress you enormously.

If you accept that you can have rules for yourself, but that other people do not have to have the same rules as you, you will find it very liberating.

You can then watch people doing things that don't seem 'right' to you, but no longer care.

And if you felt adventurous, you could even experiment with doing things the way they do them.

'The golden rule is that there are no golden rules.'

George Bernard Shaw

March 6

Letting Go

'Insecurity twists meanings and poisons trust.'

Graham Greene

Often, to counteract our insecurity, we try to control our world.

Naturally, we fail, the world is beyond our control – and in fact, if we knew it, we are beyond our control too.

When things don't go the way we would like them to, we become frustrated with ourselves, and we resent the people who are not doing things in the 'right' way.

The most we can do with either is to try to guide them in the direction we want.

If we can learn to accept that there is a natural order in the world, and learn to allow it to flow in the way it does, it will release us from our struggle to make it better.

We may still want to work on aspects of it. We may even succeed in improving some, but when life goes its own merry or miserable way, ignoring our attempts, we want to accept that.

We no longer need to suffer. We are not in control. What a relief.

'Endure this evil, lest worse come to you.'

Phaedrus

'Pain is inevitable, suffering is optional.'

Buddha

'The more he looked inside the more Piglet wasn't there.'

A A Milne

March 7

Awareness

*'As white as a candle
In a holy place,
So is the beauty
Of an aged face.'*

Joseph Campbell

So much in our world today focuses on the beauty of the young and the new. We often fail to take the time to look at, let alone see, the aged or the old.

As we get older ourselves, we tend not to look at ourselves. We may look in detail at our lips as we apply lipstick, or our cheeks as we shave. But we often fail to study the whole. We don't notice the ageing process in ourselves.

It is worthwhile to broaden our horizons to start to study the old and the familiar. To look at people, places, and things, to explore and discover the beauty in the world that surrounds us.

*'No spring, nor summer beauty hath such grace,
As I have seen in one autumnal face.'*

John Donne

March 8

Gossiping

'It will be a beautiful family talk, mean and worried and full of sorrow and spite and excitement. I cannot be asked to miss it in my weak state. I should only fret.'

Ivy Compton-Burnett

How evil it is to gossip. We weave our self-righteousness around the character assassination of others.

Like birds on the ground flicking crusts of bread in the air, then dashing over to peck at and toss the piece we've just seen landing.

It is possible to have conversations without discussing the 'shortcomings' of others.

And like all negativity, gossiping leaves a blackness in our day.

Yes, we may enjoy it, but that doesn't mean it's okay. There are lots of things that people enjoy that are not good.

If we cannot think of pleasant things to say about people, let's say nothing at all. We want to go out of our way to look for goodness.

'A sharp tongue is the only edged tool that grows keener with constant use.'

Washington Irving

'Men of few words are the best men.'

William Shakespeare – Henry V

March 9

Love

'Why do I love you? I love you not only for what you are but for what I am when I am with you. I love you not only for what you have made of yourself but for what you are making of me.'

Liberace

'I love you. I am listening.'

Sarah Blondin

The total wonder of loving, being in love and being loved.

Total absolute wonder. I wish it on the world – on everyone. And yet, sadly, I doubt that it often exists. I wish that I could give it to you as the world gives us rain and sunshine.

Sarah Blondin has an incredibly powerful meditation on Insight Timer about love, in which she asks us to say to ourselves "I love you. I am listening."

And that is a gateway to love.

If we can stop, if we can honestly say it to ourselves and listen, then we can open our hearts to love.

To truly love others, we have to be prepared to love ourselves truly.

And then – Love is.

We are open. We can receive and give.

And I want to say, to you, thank you, thank you, thank you, that I am filled with love.

'I love you because you have done so much to make me happy. You have done it without a word, without a touch, without a sign. You have done it by just being yourself. Perhaps, after all, that is what love means, and that is why I love you.'

Liberace

March 10

Spirituality

'Out of the night that covers me,
Black as the pit from pole to pole,
I thank whatever gods may be
For my unconquerable soul.'

W E Henley

We are not just bodies, pacing the earth for a short span.

We are undoubtedly more significant than that, soul or spirits inhabiting a human body, on a journey of discovery.

Take a few moments

– **Now** –

Go within, become aware of your body from within, and identify the energy, the light that is there.

Just focus on your inner self and let all thoughts drop out of your mind. You are then close to your soul. Enjoy peace and radiance.

The more often you do this, the stronger your connection will become.

It is possible to go through your day with a part of your mind focused on, aware of your inner being, your soul.

It is not possible to imagine the changes and improvements that this will bring to your life. It is only possible to experience it.

'I am positive I have a soul; nor can all the books with which materialists have pestered the world ever convince me to the contrary.'

Laurence Sterne

March 11

Growth

'Sometimes I lie awake at night and I ask , 'Where have I gone wrong?' Then a voice says to me 'This is going to take more than one night.'

Charles M Schulz – Peanuts

We all make mistakes – yes, really, we all do. Sometimes we may think that some people are perfect, that they never do anything wrong – but even they, in quiet, dark moments, question their own behaviour.

Some spend their lives beating themselves up, living in misery because of all the wrong they've done.

Most of our mistakes are not as important as we imagine them to be.

We have a choice about whether to repeat them or to use them as steppingstones to new behaviours and achievements.

If we're not making mistakes, it means that we're not doing anything that challenges us, so we are not growing.

Everything in the world is either growing or decaying.

'There is no mistake so great as the mistake of not going on.'

William Blake

March 12

Loneliness

'Throw out a life-line, throw out a life-line,
Someone is sinking today.'

Edward Smith Ufford

So easy to travel through the day in our comfortable little cocoon, oblivious of others.

And yet by saying something, by stretching out our hand, not only do we improve their lives and ours, we may make a change in the world.

'All the lonely people, where do they all come from?
All the lonely people, where do they all belong?'

Lennon & McCartney

March 13

Goals

'My country is a garden,
Such gardens are not made
By saying "Oh how beautiful."
And sitting idly in the shade.'

Rudyard Kipling

It's so easy to want something, to want to change, to want to improve oneself, to want to meditate, to want peace of mind, to want to lose weight, to want to be a success, but, so often, when it comes to it, after the first burst of enthusiasm, we somehow can't quite make the effort.

We think 'I really must do that... soon.' 'I know I will... sometime.' 'I'm so busy at the moment...' 'If only I had the time.'

Which means that it wasn't something we wanted in the first place. At least not something we 'really' wanted.

If we do want something, we need a plan. We are far more likely to succeed if we write it down. An unwritten plan is just a dream. We may do it for a while, but when we falter, we simply let it slip from our minds.

If it's written, it's a contract with ourselves, and we can go back and start again with renewed vigour.

'Nothing grows in our garden, only washing. And babies.'

Dylan Thomas

March 14

Communication

'There are some who speak one moment before they think.'

Jean de la Bruyère

Obviously, that applies to others. It would be a courageous person to admit that it referred to them.

So often people make phone calls and launch into their needs, wants, and demands, without giving a moment's thought to the person they are interrupting.

What a delight it is when someone calls us and starts by asking, 'Is this a good time to call?' or 'Am I disturbing you?' or 'Are you free to talk for a couple of minutes?'

We at once feel respected, and even if we are busy, we are far more likely to give them our attention.

It is, of course, a two-way street.

'In me the need to talk is a primary impulse, and I can't help saying right off what comes to my tongue.'

Miguel de Cervantes

March 15

Balance

'The sunlight on the garden
Hardens and grows cold,
We cannot cage the minute
Within its net of gold.'

Louis MacNeice

Because the sunlight disappears, we appreciate it. If it shone all the time, we would soon complain.

Too much of anything, good food, laughter, praise, lose their edge if that is all we experience.

We need to have the ups and downs, the failures and the triumphs, the joys and the sorrows. Otherwise, everything becomes boring.

So as we travel through time, we want to take a moment to be grateful for the difficulties, disappointments and tragedies that happen, for without them we could not enjoy our sublime moments.

'In this world, there are only two tragedies. One is not getting what one wants, and the other is getting it.'

Oscar Wilde

March 16

Criticism

'Everything is funny as long as it's happening to somebody else.'

Will Rogers

It is easy to make gentle fun of people, especially to those close to us. Sometimes the cruelty is blatant, even when everyone laughs.

'Don't give it to John – he'll drop it.'

'What do you mean a boyfriend? Mary'll never get a boyfriend.'

'You're so stupid. There you go again talking nonsense.'

~~~

Whether it's a joke or not, even if everybody laughs, and the person you're talking about laughs and 'takes it well', it makes no difference, the unconscious has no sense of humour.

So the victim's unconscious does not know that it's a joke. It hears what is said and believes that that is the way things should be. It thinks to itself 'Oh, I can drop things, I'm good at that' or 'Oh, I can make sure I never get a boyfriend, that is easy.'

So those 'funny' remarks are merely reinforcing the behaviour in the person. They are dragging the person down. (Even when the person is laughing along with everyone else.)

If we care about them, we want to stop saying it. And even if we don't, we want to stop saying it.

And we want to stop other people from saying things about us that we do not want in our lives.

'Sarcasm I now see to be, in general, the language of the devil.'

Thomas Carlyle
~~~

March 17

Language

'She looked as if she had been poured into her clothes and had forgotten to say "When".'

P G Wodehouse

Did you ever hear anyone say, 'I can't lose weight'?

People are continually saying they can't do this or that.

By saying 'can't', they abdicate their responsibility, so it's no longer their fault if they fail.

We want to replace 'can't' with 'choose not to'.

If someone were to say, 'I choose not to lose weight', don't you think that they might view their statement differently and that they might even choose to do something about it.

'I can't fly a plane'. Well, for most of us, the reason is that we haven't learnt how to fly a plane yet, rather than we can't.

Empower yourself. Discard the word can. Choose to use the word choose.

'Freedom is always and exclusively freedom for the one who thinks differently.'

Rosa Luxemburg

March 18

Expectations

'The lark now leaves his watery nest
And climbing, shakes his dewy wings;
He takes this window for the east;
And to implore your light, he sings,
Awake, awake, the morn will never rise,
Till she can dress her beauty in your eyes.'

William Davenant

Whether we awake at dawn or not, we will awaken. How do we do that? How do we feel? Do we leap from the bed with joy and anticipation, or do we steal some extra sleep? Do we drag our aching body from the bed, or do we feel rested and alive?

It has little to do with age. It has to do with the mind. And most importantly, it depends on what we expect before we go to sleep.

If we expect a sleepless night, troubled dreams and to feel exhausted in the morning, our unconscious will surely oblige.

If, before we go to sleep, we tell ourselves (and therefore our unconscious) that we want to sleep well and deeply. That we want to awake feeling refreshed, full of energy and enthusiasm, with a healthy body, it will begin to happen. I say begin because if we have had the habit of sleeping poorly, it might take a few attempts to change that.

(Don't say 'I'll feel free of aches' or 'I won't be disturbed during the night' because your unconscious won't process the negative and you'll get aches and be disturbed. Only say the things that you want.)

'Tired nature's sweet restorer, balmy sleep!'

Edward Young

March 19

Desire

'Do not let your fire go out, spark by irreplaceable spark in the hopeless swamps of the not-quite, the not-yet, and the not-at-all. Do not let the hero in your soul perish in lonely frustration for the life you deserved and have never been able to reach. The world you desire can be won. It exists... it is real... it is possible... it is yours.'

Ayn Rand

Three signposts:-

'Beware! Swamps!'

~~~

'You are in the swamp.'

~~~

'You just died in the swamp.'

~~~

There's a fourth one:-

'You can get out of the swamp – you can live.'

~~~

What we do with the rest of our lives is up to us. All choices are available. Whatever happens, the next step we take, the next thing we do, will move us towards the end.

What do we want it to be? What do we need to do to move in the direction we want?

~~~

Fifth:-

'The world you desire can be won. It exists...
it is real... it is possible... it's yours.'

'As far as we can discern, the sole purpose of human existence is to kindle a light in the darkness of mere being.'

Carl Jung
~~~

March 20

Complaints

'It is so many years before one can believe enough in what one feels even to know what the feeling is.'

W B Yeats

'I'm fine...' How many times have we lied? How many times have we avoided looking people in the eye?

Supposedly, if you tell people bad news about yourself, 60% of people couldn't care less, and 39% of people are glad you've got the trouble.

We hear someone's complaint or moan and use it as a launching pad to expound all our troubles, without even processing theirs.

And we're not even interested in what they have to say about us unless they ladle sympathy all over us.

So, when we catch ourselves saying 'I'm fine' or worse still complaining our lot, we want to pause for a moment and ask ourselves what, if anything, we are going to do about it.

Find the 1% who care about us and discuss our lives with them. Make a plan, change what we are doing, take control of our lives.

'Insanity is doing the same thing over and over again and expecting different results.'

Albert Einstein

March 21

Language

'Your prayer must be for a sound mind in a sound body.'

Juvenal

The trouble with that quote is the word must.

Must, should, have to, will do, got to, ought to, are all authority words. They are the words our parents, teachers and authority figures used. And now when we hear them, especially when we say them to ourselves, our unconscious sticks its heals in and shouts 'Get Lost' (actually probably 'F - ck off') and determines not to do it. Or if we do it, we sulk, without enjoyment, dragging our feet.

Just think/process/say out loud, 'I **must** cook supper'... How does that make you feel?

Now say 'I **ought** to cook supper.'

'I **have to** cook supper.' none of them are very appealing.

And now say 'I **want** to cook supper.' and suddenly it is an attractive idea.

(If cooking supper is something you love doing substitute the action 'I **must** take out the garbage' or 'I **must** go to work' and see how different the musts and the wants feel.)

So we want to discard the authority words from our language and replace them with the word 'want'.

Then we will achieve much more, and we will enjoy it.

'If you don't get what you want, it's a sign either that you did not seriously want it, or that you tried to bargain over the price.'

Rudyard Kipling

March 22

Guilt

'That loathsome centipede, Remorse.'

H S Leigh

Guilt can eat away at us. We re-run the video of what happened, time after time, magnifying the awfulness of it all.

That is how most people use guilt, they beat themselves up with it, and that is not guilt's job at all.

We do something, which is "less good" than it could have been, and guilt comes and taps us on the shoulder and asks, 'What do you think about what you just did?'

There are three replies we can give.

a:- 'It was fine' And if that is true, then guilt can go away.

b:- 'I know it wasn't good, I shall apologise, and I won't do it again.' Once again, guilt can leave its work is complete.

c:- 'I know it wasn't good, but I'm not ready to change at the moment, I'm going to go on doing it.' Again, guilt has done its job. If we are going to continue with the behaviour, then it is pointless to feel guilty about it. We can get on with life and enjoy it.

So it is clear from all that, that re-running the videos and beating ourselves up is just self-indulgent.

We can't change the past, but we can alter our attitudes and feelings about it. If we go around with an enormous millstone tied to our necks, we are not able to do our best, for ourselves or anyone else.

'We all piss in the swimming pool. Because I piss from the diving board, am I guilty?'

Jan Kalina

March 23

Grief

*'We cannot help the birds of sadness flying over our heads,
But we need not let them build their nests in our hair.'*

Chinese Proverb

Tragedies happen, to all of us. Some are greater than others. Disasters give us an opportunity to grow.

For us to travel through them, two things must happen.

We have to accept what has happened, and that we can't change it, life's not going to be the same again, but it will go on, as best it can.

We also want to share our troubles with others and with God.

We can decide to use our experiences to help others, and so bring light, not only into our lives but into the world.

'Human life begins on the other side of despair.'

Jean-Paul Sartre

'Happiness is beneficial for the body, but it is grief that develops the powers of the mind.'

Marcel Proust

March 24

Reality

'Not a whit, we defy augury: there's a special providence in the fall of a sparrow. If it be now; 'tis not to come, it will be now; if it be not now, yet it will come: the readiness is all.'

Willian Shakespeare – Hamlet

Life happens. And often it is uncomfortable. We want to fight it. Sometimes we want to blame it. Curse it for what it has done to us, and how we feel.

Only we can make us feel anything. We choose to feel happy, sad, lucky, unlucky. I am the only person who can create what I want. Because it is the feeling that goes with what I want, that makes it real.

When we were young, we were the centre of our universe. If bad things happened to other people, we felt it was our fault. When good things happened, it just confirmed our power over the world.

Growing out of that, realising that we are not responsible, and learning that life goes on, with or without us, can be very freeing. When we stop trying to control people, places, and things, we can lead richer, fuller, lives, and are far more likely to be able to help others.

' "Contrariwise," continued Tweedledee, "if it was so, it might be; and if it were so, it would be: but as it isn't, it ain't. That's logic." '

Lewis Carrol

March 25

Honesty

'Golf... is the infallible test. The man who can go into a patch of rough alone, with the knowledge that only God is watching him, and play his ball where it lies, is the man who will serve you faithfully and well.'

P G Wodehouse

How do we behave when no-one's watching?

What do we think that no-one can hear?

What are the images that float into our minds as we fall asleep?

'Integrity has no need of rules.'

Albert Camus

'It's easy to make a man confess the lies he tells to himself; it's far harder to make him confess the truth.'

Geoffrey Household

March 26

Worry

'Worry is interest paid on trouble before it falls due.'

W R Inge

'Worry is like praying for things you don't want.'

Michael Shook

Worry is quietly rotating the future over and over again in our minds, like a chicken being spit-roasted. There's a leg, a breast, a leg, a back, a leg, a breast. There's nothing we can do about the chicken, or the worry, until it's taken off and put on a plate.

To combat this, to stop endlessly grabbing at one thought after another, we want to know what the things are that have to be done, even if at this moment we don't know how to achieve them – and this requires a written list, otherwise, they rotate away.

Because when we have the list, we can say, what can I do now, at this moment, and then do it.

When there is nothing we can do now, we can say to ourselves, 'I can't do anything about it at the moment, there's no point in thinking about it until... ' and set a time in the future when we will take action.

Then we can put it aside and occupy our minds and bodies with something else. (Like going to sleep perhaps.)

If it does pop into our mind again we simply say to ourselves, 'I don't need to think about that, it's on the list.'

'He looked haggard and careworn, like a Borgia who has suddenly remembered that he has forgotten to shove the cyanide into the consommé and the dinner-gong is about to go.'

P G Wodehouse

March 27

Consciousness

'There are three classes of people, those who see; those who see when they are shown; those who do not see.'

Leonardo da Vinci

We tend to hurry through our lives, with our tunnel vision letting us see, hear, taste, experience only a minute amount of the world we inhabit.

Children want to experience things fully, which is why they eat earth, gaze into the distance, stick their hands into dangerous places. 'Don't! Don't!' we cry. So they become programmed to do less and less.

So here we are, grown-up, living a blinkered, unadventurous life.

Start to explore your world. Look at the buildings on your way to work, the supermarket. No! Really look at them, why have they chosen the materials they have? Listen to people and songs and think about what they mean. Experiment with new foods. Look at trees and plants. Really look at them. Look at the spaces between the leaves.

Bring adventure back into your life. Live more fully.

Not just once. Challenge yourself to add new things all the time.

'If the doors of perception were cleansed, everything would appear to man as it is, infinite.'

William Blake

March 28

Advice

'Advice is what we ask for when we already know the answer, but wish we didn't.'

Erica Jong

Most of us genuinely, from time to time, think we want advice, but more often than not, we are just seeking confirmation for the action that we have at some level already decided to take. So we go from one person to the next until we find someone that tells us what we want to hear.

In many instances, this doesn't matter, but there are times when we do need advice, and it's essential to realise in advance that we may well have to do things, which we know in our heart of hearts, we don't want to do. The sooner we decide to take the necessary action, the easier it is to do what we have to do.

Just deciding that we are going to do what we need to do, will lift a weight from our minds and give us immense freedom.

'Advice is seldom welcome; and those who want it most like it least.'

Earl of Chesterfield

March 29

Agreement

'Ah! Don't say you agree with me. When people say they agree with me, I always feel I must be wrong.'

Oscar Wilde

How easy it is to agree – when we don't. Just for simplicity's sake. Or because it's less bother.

And so, we find ourselves doing things that – given a choice – we'd prefer not to do.

How strange.

Maybe, part of the problem, is that we've either not thought about what we'd like to do, or that we haven't thought at all. And/or, because we've never learnt to tell people what we don't want to do, or what we do want to do.

So many people find their head saying, 'No', while their mouth says, 'Yes'. And the second the 'Yes' is out, we're trying to think of ways to get out of doing it.

So often there is just a silent agreement, where one complies with what <u>they</u> want because that is the way it's always been, so it is impossible to say no.

And this can be true in every area of our lives.

We want to learn to take responsibility for ourselves and discover that the world doesn't end when we say no to the things we don't want to do.

'A character, no more than a fence, cannot be strengthened by whitewash.'

Paul Frost

March 30

Anger

'Anger Holding onto anger is like grasping a hot coal with the intent of throwing it at someone else; you are the one who gets burned.'

Buddha

Nobody can make us angry. We choose to be angry. 'No!' you cry 'He made me angry!'

But it's not true. We've all experienced moments when we're driving happily along, and someone overtakes us aggressively, and we don't even notice. But on another occasion, someone overtakes us, and we're swearing away, trying to plan how we can get even.

So we choose to be angry, or we decide not to be. And when we become angry, the only person we are hurting is ourselves. Our body starts to fill with poison. 90%+ of all accidents happen because the person is angry.

Ask anyone, who has just broken something, banged into something, hurt themselves, and they will nearly always admit that they were angry before it happened.

And what is worse still, is that when we become angry, the person whom we believed caused our anger is now controlling our emotions. So now, not only are we angry, but the other person is winning, pulling our strings, directing our dance. So we want to learn to be able to take a deep breath and let the event pass us by, let ourselves cool down, allow ourselves to let go of the event, to choose calmness.

To be able to look at what's happened as if it happened to someone else, and to say to ourselves, 'Ok that wasn't great, but come on, it's not worth making it worse for ourselves, by getting angry about it.'

'He who angers you conquers you.'

Elizabeth Kenny

March 31

Deceit

'O, what a tangled web we weave,
When first we practice to deceive!'

Sir Walter Scott

Sometimes, being human, we say or do things that are, maybe, slightly less than honest.

For example, we are asked to do something, and we say we will. Maybe at that moment, we believe that we will do what we've agreed to do. Perhaps though, we've only said we will, to get some peace and to be left alone.

However, doing this drains us, and it drains them.

And when we are drained, we aren't whole.

So much better to be honest.

If we tell them that we aren't going to do it when they ask us, we may not get instant peace, but in the long run, both they and we will gain. We will both begin to know where we stand, rather than continuing to live on an unclear grey map, which no one can read.

If we deceive others, we are deceiving ourselves, and in the long run, we pay the price of our deception.

'Why are you bothering to lie to me? You are like a man on a desert island refusing to admit to his companion that he ate the last coconut.'

Tom Stoppard

Enjoying?

Share

This

Book

With

Someone

Else

April 1

Self-image

'What a bore it is waking up in the morning always the same person.'

Logan Pearsall Smith

One morning an elderly, wealthy, but ill man was making his way, in his wheelchair, from his mansion to his car. At that moment, a young, broke, healthy, man was walking past. Their eyes met, and they were both filled with envy.

It happened to be April Fool's Day, and a passing angel noticed their feelings, and in a fit of whimsy, granted their wish to trade places.

The young man's mind found itself in the ill, crippled body of the rich man, while the rich man's mind found itself in the wonderfully healthy body of the broke young man.

A few years later, they happened to pass one another again.

The young man's body was now ill, and crippled, but was rich, while the older body was healthy and, on its way, to becoming broke.

We create our worlds. Unless we learn to change our minds, nothing changes.

'We should all know what's at the end of our ropes, and how it feels to be there.'

Richard Ford

April 2

Adventure

'Whatever you may be sure of, be sure at least of this, that you are dreadfully like other people.'

James Russell Lowell

A friend tells you that their teenage son is off to spend three months living in the Amazon jungle. 'How wonderful, how brilliant.'

Your 19-year-old son announces that he is off to spend three months living in the Amazon jungle. Your heart sinks. You are overwhelmed with fear and apprehension.

Why let other people take risks for us?

Why live in a cardboard box with a cape of bubble wrap?

Why not dare?

'Most people are other people. Their thoughts are someone else's opinions, their lives a mimicry, their passions a quotation.'

Oscar Wilde

April 3

Action

'Jogging is very beneficial. It's good for your legs and your feet. It's also very good for the ground. It makes it feel needed.'

Snoopy – Charles M Schulz

Don't sit for hours. Classes in school are only 45 minutes long because they discovered the wandering mind. To continue to be productive, we want to add movement into our day.

Just a couple of minutes of brisk movement makes a difference, go to the coffee machine or wherever you like.

If we can find a way to walk a little further, to move a bit more briskly throughout the day, it will significantly improve our well-being, concentration and productivity.

If we can take real exercise, that's even better. But we still want to break the day into segments and have movement.

'The sovereign invigorator of the body is exercise, and of all exercises, walking is the best.'

Thomas Jefferson

'A bear, however hard he tries,
Grows tubby without exercise.'

A A Milne

April 4

Change

'When a man is determined, what can stop him? Cripple him and you have a Sir Walter Scott. Put him in a prison cell and you have a John Bunyan. Bury him in the snows of Valley Forge and you have a George Washington. Have him born in abject poverty and you have a Lincoln. Put him in the grease pit of a locomotive roundhouse and you have a Walter P Chrysler. Make him second fiddle in an obscure South African orchestra and you have a Toscanini. The hardships of life are sent not to be an unkind destiny to crush, but to challenge.'

Sam E Roberts

Life is what we make it. We choose. We decide whether to continue with our experience, or whether to change it.

It is scary to change. It is so easy to stay with what we know. Whatever we have chosen, we want to accept.

If we put sugar in our coffee but do not stir it, whose fault is it if our coffee is bitter?

'Cathedrals cannot be built by those who are paralysed by doubt and cynicism.'

Henry Kissinger

April 5

Meditation

' "Isn't that lovely" she sighed. "It's my favourite program – fifteen minutes of silence – and after that there's a half hour of quiet and then an interlude of lull." '

Norton Juster

Silence. How wonderful. To escape from the endless chatter – of one's mind.

You can achieve this by learning to concentrate on your breathing and so escape from your thoughts.

Here is a meditation to do just that, and the benefits are magnificent!

Sit comfortably. Relax your body.

1 Breathe in - Breathe out count 1
Continue until 10, Start again at 1
Repeat for a period of time

Just be aware of breathing and counting, if/when your mind wanders off (into chatter) bring it gently back to your breath and counting.

2 Be aware of your body rising and falling as you breathe in and out

3 Be aware of the breath as it enters then leaves your body.

That's it. Ideally, each stage wants to last for roughly the same length of time. The idea is to concentrate on the breathing and to learn to escape from your thoughts.

Start with a few minutes, and you can gradually increase to more extended periods of peace.

Too busy to meditate?

It's worth every second of it.

'Silence is the perfectest herald of joy: I were but little happy if I could say how much.'

William Shakespeare – Much Ado About Nothing

April 6

Giving

'In the west people make free with words like 'freedom' and 'the spirit', but few ever think to ask a man whether he has enough money for lunch.'

Czeslaw Milosz

There are those less fortunate than us. And now we are not just approached by beggars, but we are approached by the money-raising clip-boarders, trolling for charity.

So it is not surprising that many of us withdraw from giving, finding banal excuses which don't even convince ourselves.

And to top it all, there are those who 'beg us' for emotional support when we may feel that our needs are more significant than theirs and that to give any more would completely drain us.

What can we do? However ever badly off we are, there are people with greater needs than ours. And by giving what we can, willingly, with generosity, the reward will be infinitely more than the cost to us. It may be that we have to budget what we can give today. Then we can look for opportunities for charity with inner joy. And know that when we turn someone away, it is because we have already, honestly given.

Whatever we give, we receive back many times that gift, usually from a completely different source. There may be times that we cannot give money, but whatever our circumstances are, we can always give praise. The gift of praise is magnificent.

'I try to give to the poor people for love what the rich could get for money. No, I wouldn't touch a leper for a thousand pounds; yet I willingly cure him for the love of God'

Mother Teresa

April 7

Individuality

'In Berlin, we say you should leave another man's moustache alone, even if it droops into his coffee cup.'

Phillip Kerr

How wonderful to be able to accept the characteristics of others without judgement.

How splendid to be able to enjoy our peculiarities without embarrassment.

There may be things that we do, that it would be best to do in private, but if we choose to go out in a 'funny' hat, let's enjoy ourselves. Whatever we do, we must not apologise for our hat.

We spend so much of our life conforming, living within the mundane norm of society. When we defy convention, we bring a little light into the world. The world needs more fun.

'I love a man with a moustache. And luckily for me, I've found a man who loves a woman with one.'

Barbara Pike

April 8

Friends

'If a man does not make new acquaintances as he advances through life, he will soon find himself left alone. A man, Sir, should keep his friendship in constant repair.'

Samuel Johnson

Why is it that we fail to make new friends? Some people feel they are inadequate, and they think that everyone else is more successful, better, more intelligent and that if they were to attempt to approach others, they would face rejection. The other side of the coin is that they feel more intelligent and generally superior, and so to contemplate making friends with others would be a waste of time.Both these thoughts are created by fear.

Suppose we take a risk, and dare to say some opening words in a conversation to someone we barely know – what then? Does the world end? It may take an incredible effort on our part – but so what.

Generally, some sort of conversation happens, and it peters out, and we move on. But sometimes we strike gold and find the birth of a friendship. Like all prospectors, we have to mine in many places before we can have success. But the rewards are priceless.

'My life is spent in a perpetual alternation between two rhythms, the rhythm of attracting people for the fear I may be lonely, and the rhythm of trying to get rid of them because I know that I am bored.'

C E M Joad

'My mother used to say that there were no strangers, only friends you haven't met yet. She's now in a maximum-security twilight home in Australia.'

Dame Edna Everage

April 9

Health

'Illness is not something a person has. It's another way of being.'

Jonathan Miller

'If there was one thing he hated more than another it was the way she had of waking him in the morning... It was her way of establishing her grievance for the day.'

Katherine Mansfield

Some of us are better at bearing illness, pain, and discomfort than others. Some are good at choosing not to be ill.

Recently an office experienced a flu epidemic, half the staff were waged, and the rest were self-employed, the paid employees all caught the flu, while the self-employed did not.

I know people who've had continuous operations and live in constant pain, but to meet them, you simply would not know.

How we respond to illness and hardship is our choice. And often whether we succumb to it or not, is also our choice.

If we are choosing to be ill, it makes sense to wonder why?

'Tragedy is when I cut my finger – comedy is when you walk into an open sewer and die.'

Mel Brooks

April 10

Control

'He that overvalues himself will undervalue others, and he that undervalues others will oppress them.'

Samuel Johnson

'He that would govern others, first should be, master of himself.

Philip Massinger

We may like to think we can control others, but we cannot. True we may be able to enforce our rules on them, but only for as long as they obey. We don't want to waste our time focusing on preventing others from making mistakes and doing the things we do not want them to do.

In truth, we have a big enough challenge controlling ourselves, and that is where we want to spend our energies.

If we can have self-control and freedom at the same time, we may consider that we are becoming miraculous.

The difference between an ordinary person and a genius is that geniuses use their brains differently. As long as we are pursuing self-improvement, we are using our minds differently.

'But what if I should discover that the least among them all, the poorest of all beggars, the most impudent of all offenders, yea the very fiend himself - that these are within me, and that I myself stand in need of my own kindness, that I myself am the enemy who must be loved - what then?'

Carl Jung

April 11

Living

'This is the true joy of life, the being used for a purpose recognised by yourself as a mighty one; the being thoroughly worn out before you are thrown on the scrap heap; the being a force of Nature instead of a feverish, selfish little clod of ailments and grievances complaining that the world will not devote itself to making you happy.'

George Bernard Shaw

We might ask ourselves, what have I done in the last 24 hours to make a difference? Or perhaps, even more usefully, what am I going to do in the next 24 hours to make a difference?

That is the sort of question that tends to make the mind go blank.

Perhaps we need to set aside some quiet time to consider this, view the world, and the people we encounter with an attitude of 'What can I do for you?'

Rather than 'What is in this for me?'

Don't let us use any old excuse not to review our life choices.

'The purpose of life is not to be happy. It is to be useful, to be honourable, to be compassionate, to have it make some difference that you have lived and lived well.'

Ralph Waldo Emerson

April 12

Decisions

'The man who is denied the opportunity of taking decisions of importance, begins to regard as important the decisions he is allowed to take.'

C Northcote Parkinson

Are you living "because of"?

Are you doing a job because of a decision you made when you were young?

Are you in a marriage because you got into a relationship with someone whom you did not really know?

Would you go to someone now, who is the age you were when you made your career or marriage decisions, for advice on anything remotely as important as that?

Are you still in it because of the children?

Do you do things, watch things, put up with things because it's easier, or it's what you've always done?

If you even vaguely think yes to any of those questions, then do yourself a favour, take stock of your life and begin to decide what you actually want to be doing with it.

It is really important for your true well-being, that you enjoy your life. Give yourself the freedom to do it.

'The value of life lies not in the length of days but in the use you make of them; he has lived for a long time who has little lived. Whether you have lived enough depends not on the number of your years but on your will.'

Montaigne

'It is only with the heart that one can see rightly; what is essential is invisible to the eye.

Antoine de Saint-Exupéry

April 13th

Loveliest of trees, the cherry now
Is hung with bloom along the bough,
And stands about the woodland ride
Wearing white for Eastertide.

Now, of my threescore years and ten,
Twenty will not come again,
And take from seventy springs a score,
It only leaves me fifty more.

And since to look at things in bloom
Fifty springs are little room,
About the woodlands I will go
To see the cherry hung with snow.

AE Housman

April 14

Inventory

'What is hell?'
Hell is oneself,
Hell is alone, the other figures in it
Merely projections. There is nothing to escape from
And nothing to escape to. One is always alone.'

T S Elliot

A wise thing to do is to recognise the path to hell before one gets there.

An excellent way to do this is to review one's day and see if we are taking any of the roads that might lead there. If we bear some of the following questions in mind, we might be able to spot what is going on.

Today, have I interacted with people or have I isolated myself? Have I looked after myself, mentally, physically, spiritually? What did I enjoy today? Have I done things I wish I hadn't done? Do I feel proud of my day? What would I like to change, or do tomorrow, to make it better than today?

If we take a little time doing a check-up, then there is no need to descend. It is much easier to change things before they happen than afterwards.

'There may be Peace without Joy, and Joy without Peace, but the two combined make Happiness.'

John Buchan

April 15

Perspective

'Everything has been figured out, except how to live.'

Jean-Paul Sartre

It is never going to be perfect. We are never going to be perfect.

Maybe, from time to time, we need to step back, take a breath, and remember that.

Then, it may be easier to accept some of the things that have been troubling us.

'Life is tough. Three out of three people die, so shut up and deal.'

Ring Lardner

April 16

Patience

'You can learn many things from children. How much patience you have, for instance.'

Franklin P Jones

Patience is a virtue. We are all tested from time to time. We don't need children to find ourselves gritting our teeth, either metaphorically or physically.

People, that we have been around for a long time, often stretch our patience enormously, and the chances are, that we continue to suppress our feelings for far longer than is good for us, or our relationship.

It is good to clear the air – to share our frustrations, rather than letting them fester. The longer we wait, the more straws we're adding to the camel's back. And we don't want to snap.

It's also worth remembering that it's not just us who's suffering – they are too because if we're not honest with them, then we're withdrawing part of ourselves from the relationship and that affects everyone involved.

We spring clean our homes to keep our surroundings in order, so we want to do the same with our mental surroundings.

'It is not because things are difficult that we don't dare; it is because we do not dare that they are difficult.'

Lucius Annaeus Seneca

April 17

Rest

'Nothing to do but work,
Nothing to eat but food,
Nothing to wear but clothes
To keep one from going nude.'

Benjamin Franklin King

Work. Work. Work. The same old drudge time after time. Especially if our job happens to be 'just a housewife'. No breaks there.

Sometimes we need a real day off, a day when we do nothing. Just veg out and recuperate.

Even God put his feet up at the end of the week. Could there be a clue in that?

Our main difficulty is allowing ourselves to do it, and if we live with others, is preparing them for it, so that they know that they'll have to find their own socks. Or that they can, if they so choose, go without any!

The point about a day off is to do nothing, just to have the time and space to sit or lie and enjoy oneself, unbattered by the world and its occupants, a time to replenish oneself, to feel refreshed.

'Teach us to care and not to care
Teach us to sit still.'

T S Eliot

April 18

Intimacy

'I get by with a little help from my friends.'

John Lennon

Sharing with others, enjoying the areas we have in common, accepting our differences, bonds us to together. Daring to have that intimacy, to tell others who we really are, enriches us.

It is easy to hide our true self, and it is only through opening up and taking the risk of talking about who we are, that we grow.

Intimacy invites intimacy. And discovering that others have secrets and that they accept us with our shortcomings, frees us so that we live fuller, happier lives.

'A friend is a person with whom I may be sincere. Before him, I may think aloud.'

Ralph Waldo Emerson

April 19

Self-awareness

'No, when the fight begins within himself,
A man's worth something.'

Robert Browning

We've all passed a tramp talking/muttering to himself. He is just doing out loud, what we are all doing in our heads. Our ego talks endlessly to us, carrying on about the past and the future. Our mind is doing anything it can to prevent us from experiencing the present moment.

If you doubt that, just listen.

Listen to what it's saying, listen carefully, watch it.

If you do this, it will change the talk. It takes away the ego's strength. When we become the observer of the dialogue, the prattle loses its power over us.

As we continue to remove ourselves from it and become the watcher, it will diminish.

We will cease to be consumed by it, and we will be able to experience what is happening in our lives, with new freedom.

'The one self-knowledge worth having is to know one's own mind.'

F H Bradley

April 20

Humility

'And when I'm finally called, by the Great Architect, and he says, "What did you do?" I shall just bring me book out and say, "Here you are mate add that lot up." '

Tony Hancock

It's so easy to look down on people. Even the drunk alcoholic, who may often feel on a par with a piece of cat shit in the gutter, can manage to look down on others.

And if that's the case, then how much easier it is for us.

As we get older, our disapproval and judgement of others often increases.

We are no more important than anyone else. We want to learn to recognise the rightness of others and to walk with everyone, experiencing the same road, the same dust, the same weather.

Just because we have an umbrella and they don't doesn't make us better than them, luckier maybe. More hardworking perhaps. But that can all change. We are them, and they are us. We travel as equals.

'I believe that the first test of a truly great man is his humility. I don't mean by humility, doubt of his power. But really great men have a curious feeling that the greatness is not of them, but through them. And they see something divine in every other man and are endlessly, foolishly, incredibly merciful.'

John Ruskin

April 21

Self-acceptance

'If you can't get a compliment any other way, pay yourself one.'

Mark Twain

Some of us go through life, seeking approval for everything, from everybody.

Many of us don't need that much, but we still crave it. We do our best to get our children, partners, family, friends, and workmates to say what a 'wonderful job' we've done.

When we realise that self-acceptance and personal pride in what we do are all we need, we can breathe a sigh of relief, and get on with the enjoyment of finding things in others to praise – no longer requiring their approval for our actions.

'Finding out who you are is the first step. Accepting who you are can be the hard part. Enhancing who you are is the fun part.'

B'anne Yonker

April 22

Self-awareness

'His opinion of himself, having once risen, remained at "set fair".'

Arnold Bennett

Complacency. The trouble is that the more we suffer from this, the less we realise it. We are so focused on ourselves, with self-centredness, self-pity, self-seeking, blame, etc., that we do not recognise it, and perhaps even think that there is nothing wrong with us.

It is all 'Their fault' – 'I do this and that for them' – 'What appreciation do I get?' – 'If only they understood/cared!' – 'I'm doing everything I can, what more do they want?'

All of this, however debasing it may appear, stems from pride, self-pride and an excessive need for recognition.

If we can honestly look at the situation from a perspective other than our own, and begin to realise that we, not they, are the problem, then we can start to change the way things are.

Once we have accepted this, it is a great relief, for as long as they are the problem, as long as they are 'doing it to us' there's nothing we can do. We're stuck with it.

But realising that we and the way we behave is the problem, frees us to take charge and change.

'It isn't that they can't see the solution. It is that they can't see the problem.'

G K Chesterton

April 23

Irritation

'When struck by a thunderbolt, it is unnecessary to consult the Book of Dates as to the precise meaning of the omen.'

Ernest Bramah

Fortunately, that doesn't happen too often. But little irritations occur regularly and can bother us like midges on a summers evening unless we wear insect repellant.

When we are there, unguarded, a vast expanse of naked flesh, any little noise, smell, action can bug us if we let it. 'The smell of the fast-food place across the road.' 'The people blowing their horn.' 'The mindless nonsense that people talk.' 'The fact that we've run out of....', can all bite us, poison our minds.

In the grand scheme of things, we know they're unimportant, and yet.... and yet.... they can really get to us.

If we choose to practice the art of Judo, which as I understand it, is 'Not being there when someone hits us' then the blow goes straight by. If we let 'the car horn, the smell, the nonsense' float by, then it doesn't hit us. We're not there. We become transparent. Irritations can only land if we invite them.

And why would we choose to do that?

'I wish I could care what you do or where you go but I can't.... my dear, I don't give a damn.'

Margaret Mitchell

April 24

Oneness

'That corpse you planted last year in your garden,
Has it begun to sprout? Will it bloom this year?'

T S Eliot

To be whole, we cannot just bury our pains and troubles. We cannot just replace them with activities, or pleasure, or destruction, or by filling the moment.

To be whole, we have to go inside ourselves, find oneness with our inner being, the Universal Light, our God, and allow the peace that exists, to flow through us.

Not easy to do, when shit's happening. (If my choice of words offends you, I am sorry that you're offended.) But when we're in it, we're in it, and we might as well acknowledge that.

To achieve serenity is like getting the swallows to sit on the wire. Now they're here, now they've gone, now they're back. We want to keep working towards it, grabbing it when we can, again and again.

Some of us need outside help to get rid of our emotional baggage, but whether we do or not, most of our journey is going to be alone.

We want to learn to go inside and let our troubles float away, like the dew in the morning sun, becoming aware of our inner being, our inner peace, and our love.

'If grass can grow through cement, love can find you at every time in your life.'

Cher

'I felt as if I were walking with destiny, and that all my past life had been but a preparation for this hour and for this trial.'

Winston Churchill

April 25

Envy

'If something pleasant happens to you, don't forget to tell it to your friends, to make them feel bad.'

Casimir, Comte de Montrond

There's a part of us that wants to be admired, envied even, by others.

And there's often a part of us that looks at others and what they've got and we feel envious.

Is envy bad? In moderation, probably not. We may even use it as a tool to motivate us to greater things. But it is fundamentally a negative emotion, and if it is uncontrolled, it will undoubtedly harm us and our relationships.

It can creep up on us and increase, without our even noticing it, until it starts to damage us.

When we think about it logically, we can see the stupidity in it, but emotions are not logical.

So if we are suffering, it's good to be grateful for what we have, it could be worse, and it makes sense to be happy for others.

'Waste no more time arguing what a good man should be. Be one.'

Marcus Aurelius

April 26

Excuses

'An excuse is worse and more terrible than a lie, for an excuse is a lie guarded.'

Pope John Paul II

A man asked his neighbour if he could borrow his bicycle. 'No,' replied the neighbour, 'I'm afraid not, my wife is making spaghetti bolognese for supper.' 'What has spaghetti bolognese got to do with your bicycle?' 'Nothing, but one excuse is as good as another.'

It's so easy to find ourselves giving excuses to people. But far worse is when we give excuses to ourselves.

We know they're lies, but depending on the size of the lie, we either can't be bothered to take control of our lives and do something about it, or we are simply too frightened to act.

'I attribute my success to this – I never gave or took an excuse.'

Florence Nightingale

April 27

Tolerance

'A healthy male adult bore consumes each year one and a half times his own weight in other people's patience.'

John Updike

I have a neighbour who whistles. I don't like whistling at the best of times. I particularly hate bad repetitive whistling. I feel that I cannot say anything about it to him, it might make him whistle even more – who can tell. I could play music to drown out the whistling – but I don't want to play music.

I have birds that sing. I love their songs, their songs are repetitive, but I love them all the same. Sometimes they sing, and I don't hear them singing, because I am busy doing something else. In fact, I very rarely stop what I'm doing and listen consciously. I let their songs wash around me without really noticing them.

I realised this one day. So now when I hear my neighbour whistling, I don't let my hackles rise. I don't listen to each note with anger and hatred. I choose to allow it to float past me, for the most part, unnoticed. Sometimes I remember my anger, it pops its head up, and I say to myself, 'Why would I want to feel anger?' I wouldn't, it's not nice, so I don't.

'If you cannot mould yourself as you would wish, how can you expect other people to be entirely to your liking.'

Thomas à Kempis

April 28

Happiness

'No pleasure is worth giving up for the sake of two more years in a geriatric home in Weston-Super-Mare.'

Kingsley Amis

'Pleasure is not happiness. It has no more importance than a shadow following a man.'

Muhammed Ali

Many people confuse pleasure with happiness.

We get pleasures (hopefully) from the world, the things we experience and do. But it is possible, in fact not uncommon, for people to have an abundance of pleasures and not be happy.

Happiness comes from within us. Happiness exists when we are secure within ourselves, when we enjoy inner peace and are spiritually open.

We do not need external things to be happy.

We want to share our happiness with others and allow it to grow.

'Happiness is when what you think, what you say, and what you do are in harmony.'

Mahatma Gandhi

'I was happy but happy is an adult word. You don't have to ask a child about happy, you see it. They are or they are not. Adults talk about being happy because largely they are not.'

Jeanette Winterson

April 29

Self-acceptance

'Nobody realises that some people expend tremendous energy merely to be normal .'

Albert Camus

Some people spend tremendous energy trying to be different, in so doing they simply become normal, they just don't realise it.

Some people spend their time looking down on others they consider to be normal, because, heaven forbid, they don't want to be like them.

While others are happy to just muddle along with everybody else, doing their own thing, at ease around people. Although in their heart of hearts, they know they are special and different.

The Australian comedian Barry Humphries tore the suburban Australians to shreds. He'd have couples approach him, who were the butt of his jokes, saying how much they loved his work, but they were too embarrassed to show it to their neighbours because they would be offended.

Maybe we should just be happy to be who we are, be happy for others to be who they are, and not be scared of an overlap?

'The only normal people are the ones you don't know very well.'

Alfred Adler

April 30

Focus

'Never fear shadows, they simply means there's a light somewhere nearby.'

Ruth E Renkee

Life is a roller coaster. For some of us, it's a relatively flat roller coaster, more like undulating hills. But wherever we are on the scale, we all have ups and downs. We have times of darkness and of light.

And sometimes the downs get to us. (We're human after all.)

At moments like that, it's good to pause, stop, be in the present moment, and let in the light.

Let the light fill you. Brilliant White Light.

You may say, 'When I feel really down, I can't do that.' However, if you go into yourself, into this second, everything else falls away. And if in this second you let in the light, then you'll have had a second of light and peace and strength. And you can choose to have another.

And begin to journey out of the darkness into the light.

You don't have to be really down to do this, enjoy an uplift whenever you want. Make the good even better!

'There is a crack in everything
That's how the light gets in.'

Leonard Cohen

May 1

Friends

'Friendship is always a sweet responsibility, never an opportunity.'

Kahlil Gibran

My behaviour towards others is my responsibility.

If we review our relationships honestly, we realise that we do not and should not have power over other people.

However, as we are so important to ourselves, it is easy to make the mistake of believing that we are just as important to others.

Seldom do we stop to consider that what happens to us does not concern or interest the vast majority of other people. They are focused on themselves, and so our existence is far less important to them than we might imagine.

This is true, even within a marriage.

If we do wish to improve our lives and their lives, the best way is through openness, honesty, and humility. Take the time to be interested in them, rather than taking them for granted.

'You can't hold a man down without staying down with him.'

Booker T Washington

May 2

Happiness

'When I was five years old, my mother always told me that happiness was the key to life. When I went to school, they asked me what I wanted to be when I grew up. I wrote down happy. They told me I didn't understand the assignment, and I told them they didn't understand life.'

John Lennon

How many of us have forgotten that we wanted to be happy? How many of us just accept the status quo in our lives, without thought, without ever considering that it could be better.

Of course, just considering that it might be better, won't make any difference. The only way to make a difference is to take action. To make changes, to do things differently.

What those changes might be, only we know, although it is true that sometimes we need help to realise – a:- that it is possible and b:- to discover what we could do.

If we don't want any changes, all we need to do is to continue with our lives as they are without complaint.

'Life is what happens to you while you're busy making other plans.'

John Lennon

May 3

Addiction

'In this country, don't forget, a habit is no damn private hell. There's no solitary confinement outside of jail. A habit is hell for those you love.'

Billie Holiday

'Every form of addiction is bad, no matter whether the narcotic be alcohol or morphine or idealism.'

Carl Jung

We all know people who are addicted, in one way or another. Addiction is a mental and physical illness. It's not a case of being evil or weak-willed.

When the Army officer uncle says, 'Pull yourself together' the addict replies 'I would if I could! Do you think I want to do this, to feel like this, alone, filled with feelings of wickedness, self-hatred, self-disgust.'

Addiction is an illness of isolation. The addict hides his behaviour, lies and cheats. Practically the only way to quit is to join some organisation such as Alcoholics / Narcotics / Gamblers / Cocaine / Over-Eaters Anonymous.

The addict needs to be with fellow sufferers, people he/she cannot lie to, who know when he's being dishonest, because they've been there and done it themselves.

We cannot make the addict go there, but we can leave signposts, and we can withdraw our support, as our support only enables them to continue their addiction.

'It [bingeing] gives you a feeling of comfort. It's like having a pair of arms around you, but it's temporarily, temporary. Then you're disgusted at the bloatedness of your stomach, and then you bring it all up again.'

Diana, Princess of Wales

May 4

Experience

'When men were all asleep the snow came flying,
In large white flakes falling on the city brown.'

Robert Bridges

I was sitting in my office talking to an American businessman who had come to see me when I realised I had lost him. He was looking out of the window transfixed.

It was snowing.

'Can I go out… and touch it?… I've never seen snow… '

So we went out and delighted.

When I was 18, I went with a school party to the sea. There was a boy, in my class who had never seen the sea, although in England it's not possible to be more than 70 miles from the sea.

It is so easy to assume that others have had the same experiences that we have had and take things for granted.

It's also easy to assume that because we have done something once, we know all about it, that there is nothing new to experience.

If we want to delight ourselves – and why wouldn't we – we can choose to experience things for the first time, each time.

'The dragon-green, the luminous, the dark.
The serpent-haunted sea.'

James Elroy Flecker

May 5

Change

'Science may have found a cure for most evils; but it has found no remedy for the worst of them all – the apathy of human beings.'

Helen Keller

Often, we make promises to ourselves, and nothing happens, we lack resolve, commitment, and a plan for their achievement. It is just wishful thinking.

For changes to happen, it may be that we need to discuss them with someone else, and to make a genuine commitment to do them.

It is wise to limit one's promises to a day. Forever and never are both dauntingly large, too scary, often unachievable.

'I'm never going to drink again' creates a desolate expanse of the future. It also makes us want a drink even more because we are denying ourselves a drink – forever!

Whereas most of us could make it through today without drinking and recommit tomorrow, strengthened by today's success.

(Drinking is just a metaphor for the challenges in life.)

'Let it begin with me.'

Quaker Saying

May 6

Behaviour

'The trouble is, whenever I meet anybody, they're always on their best behaviour. And when one is on one's best behaviour, one isn't at one's best.'

Alan Bennett

How well we behave with the people we know less well.

And yet often we are bored, angry, impatient, ungrateful, lazy, unpleasant, with those closest to us.

How strange.

If we were to see someone behaving like that, what would we think of them?

Our behaviour may not be particularly bad, but is it as good as it could be?

How do we want people to think of us? What do we need to do, or change, to achieve this?

'There is probably no man living, though ever so great a fool, that cannot do <u>something</u> or other well.'

Samuel Warren

May 7

Freedom

'Our experts describe you as an appallingly dull fellow, unimaginative, timid, lacking in initiative, spineless, easily dominated, no sense of humour, tedious company and irresistibly drab and awful. And whereas in most professions these would be considerable drawbacks, in chartered accountancy they are a positive boon.'

Monty Python's Flying Circus

We are not the job we do. We are not a mistake we made. We are not where we live.

There may be attributes we have, because of what we do, or did, but we are not locked into them. We are free to choose who we are today, and tomorrow, because both are new, so we may choose to behave as elegantly as we wish.

Others may indeed label us. But we do not need to live within that label. Only we can control what we think and what we choose to believe about ourselves.

'Freedom is an indivisible word. If we want to enjoy it, and fight for it, we must be prepared to extend it to everyone, whether they are rich or poor, whether they agree with us or not, no matter what their race or the colour of their skin.

Wendell Willkie

'If you can keep playing tennis when somebody is shooting a gun down the street, that's concentration. I didn't grow up playing at the country club.'

Serena Williams

May 8

Prayer

'Battering the gates of heaven with storms of prayer.'

Alfred Lord Tennyson

How do we pray? Is it abcdefghijklmno, rattled through, silently and without thought?

Is that praying?

Surely it would be better to pick one thing to pray about and concentrate on that with passion and conviction.

If we are going to recite prayers, we want to say them slowly, preferably aloud and with thought.

If we want to pray for somebody or something, we want to see them well and happy and bathed in Light.

Prayer is action.

If we want to pray for something and help it to become a reality, we want to schedule what we are going to do and when we are going to do it.

'God bless Mother and Daddy, my brother and sister, and save the king. And, Oh God, do take care of yourself, because if anything happens to you, we're all sunk.'

Adlai Stevenson – A child's prayer

May 9

Possessions

'The goal of all inanimate objects is to resist man and ultimately defeat him.'

Russell Baker

We cling to things. Things we will never use, wear, or read again. 'But just maybe... it's possible... I know I probably won't... But still... I'm so fond... Maybe next time I'm having clear out... Oh and look at that!... I haven't seen that for ages...'

If only..., if only..., if only... we could have the courage to discard, to make space in our lives, to make space in our home.

Even if we are unaware of it, objects clutter not only our space but our minds.

In my 20's, I built a 30-foot yacht which I sailed to the Canaries, where it blew up. Instead of a boat, all I had left, washed up on a beach, was a couple of hundredweight of charcoal. I realised that two things I missed were my belt and my fountain pen. Both of which I was able to replace.

What are your two things?

If we clear our space, not only do we have freedom, – but we can also go out and buy something new and glorious to enjoy.

'How many things I can do without!'

Socrates 469-399 BC.

'Have nothing in your houses that you do not know to be useful , or believe to be beautiful.'

William Morris

May 10

Change

'Having a character that consists merely of defects, I try to correct them one by one, but there are limits to the altitude that can be attained by hauling on one's own boot-straps.'

Clive James

Change requires action. It is no good just thinking about it. Prayer also requires action, merely praying and not following the prayer up with action rarely accomplishes anything.

If we do not like things the way they are, then we want to work out the things that need to change to make it better.

The only person I can change is me. I cannot change you, my friend, my partner, my children. If they are to change, it is up to them.

When we do change, the whole world changes too. Our behaviour helps to create the behaviour of others.

So we decide what needs to be different. We start by taking action to change ourselves, and – and this is important – we continue with the new behaviour. It is no good to sweep a room once and assume it will be clean forever. We need to sweep it routinely. And (this is important too) we want to enjoy doing the new thing(s).

Even if we don't enjoy them, we want to enjoy the fact we are doing them.

Just an inner smile will do.

When we find a way to enjoy it, it becomes easier to continue.

'I wanted to change the world. But I found the only thing one can change is oneself.'

Aldous Huxley

May 11

Consciousness

'I am a camera with its shutter open, quite passive, recording, not thinking.'

Christopher Isherwood

We do the same things every day, over and over again, without thought. We travel through our lives not really participating, not seeing, not touching, not smelling, not feeling, just existing.

If we can decide to do at least one thing today (and then every day) with our full attention, the ripples of consciousness, experience, and living will flow through our lives, and enrich our existence.

We can choose anything. It doesn't matter what but do it with full consciousness.

Peel a potato, walk down a passage, travel on a train or in a car for a few minutes, becoming aware of everything you are doing and everything that is happening.

Eat a mouthful of food, talk to someone, kiss someone, listen to music.

What we choose to focus on is irrelevant, what matters is that we give it our full attention and the total awareness of as many senses as possible.

Enrich yourself.

'The meanest floweret of the vale,
The simplest note that swells the gale
The common sun, the air, the skies,
To him are opening paradise.'

Thomas Grey

May 12

Eating

'When Rabbit said, "Honey or condensed milk with your bread?" he was so excited that he said, "Both," and then so as not to seem greedy, he added, "But don't bother about the bread, please." '

A A Milne

Many of us eat more than we want to. However, some people appear to eat what they want, without overindulging or putting on weight.

It hardly seems fair.

The main difference between the majority, and the naturally slender person, is that before the naturally slim person eats, they don't think about immediate gratification, they unconsciously travel forwards in their mind 3 or 4 hours and ask themselves these questions.

How will I feel then if I eat nothing now?

How will I feel then if I eat 'this' (an apple) now?

How will I feel then if I eat 'something else' (a doughnut) now?

Their decision about what and whether to eat now, is based on how they will feel in 3 or 4 hours.

And they continue this process while eating, so if halfway through their plate of food, they realise that they'll feel less good in the future if they continue to eat, they stop.

With a little practice and perseverance, this process is open to anyone.

'She fitted into my biggest armchair as if it had been built round her by someone who knew they were wearing armchairs tight about the hips that season.'

P G Wodehouse

May 13

Gratitude

'The obligation of gratitude may easily become a trap, and the young are often caught and maimed in it.'

Eric Gill

I seem to remember hearing "Develop an Attitude of Gratitude." And no doubt I thought yes – if I thought at all – and moved on.

And yet we do want to be overwhelmed with gratitude. Not to people, although that's good unless as in the quote above, we become their prisoners. We want to be overwhelmed with gratitude to life, to being, to existing.

We want to rejoice in our emotions, delight that we are here to have them, fly through our time here, doing cartwheels in the sky, feel our gratitude filling us and bursting out of us like a shaken drinks can exploding.

And we want to share it with others whenever and wherever we can.

There may be times, in our lives, of bleak blackness, but they are just steppingstones, in our grand adventure. When we tread on one, rather than looking down, and being dragged down by it, we want to gaze up at our horizons, be grateful for their light, and move on.

'I shall remember while the light lives yet,
And in the night time I shall not forget.'

A C Swinburne

'Do not complain about growing old, it's a privilege denied to many.'

Mark Twain

May 14

Memory

'Oh, the wild joys of living! The leaping from rock up to rock,
The strong rending of boughs from the fir-tree, the cool silver shock
Of the plunge in a pool's living water.'

Robert Browning

We don't need to see the sun beyond the clouds to know it's there.

We don't need to look out of the window, or walk in the country, to feel the breeze, smell the wild, and lose ourselves in its wonder.

We just need to know that they exist and let our mind transport us.

'Very little is needed to make a happy life; it is all within yourself, in your way of thinking.'

Marcus Aurelius

May 15

Awareness

'What makes the desert beautiful is that somewhere it hides a well.'

Antoine de Saint-Exupéry

The world is full of beauty, and we are always surrounded by it, immersed in it. Not only in those things we see, hear, feel, taste, but also in the actions of people.

If we did not know, if we don't accept, the fact that there is a well in the desert, we can walk right past the well and not see, taste, smell, or bathe in it.

It is up to us to choose what we perceive in any situation.

We can decide to live in the wonder that surrounds us, glory in it, and share its magnificence with others.

'A thing of beauty is a joy forever;
Its loveliness increases; it will never
Pass into nothingness.'

John Keats

May 16

Borrowing

'The louder he talked of his honour, the faster we counted our spoons.'

Ralph Waldo Emerson

Sometimes we 'borrow' things, a book, an umbrella, a pen, a spoon, a cup of sugar, or even bigger things.

How do we feel when people 'borrow' from us? Does it bother us?

Do we borrow things mindlessly ourselves?

Some people get very upset when things go missing.

Has the time to give it a thought arrived?

Most of the time, we just journey on, without thinking about it, as we jot something down with 'his' pen.

Maybe we would feel 'cleaner' if we did return it.

Perhaps none of this matters, and we'll just carry on regardless, who will know or care.

But we know. We have to decide whether we care.

'The rain it raineth every day
Upon the just and unjust feller
But more upon the just than unjust,
Because the unjust has the just's umbrella.'

Charles Bowen

May 17

Letting go

'Even a happy life cannot be without a measure of darkness, and the word "happiness" would lose its meaning if it were not balanced by sadness.'

Carl Jung

We can often laugh today at the disasters that happened eight years, eight months or even eight days ago.

We laugh to move on, to complete the circle, to close out the awfulness of the event.

We all have good and bad times, and we can choose which we remember, which we dwell on.

Even if we cannot laugh at the past, we can move on from it. We can cease to be the prisoners of unhappy memories. As long as we dwell on them, we deny ourselves the ability to live and enjoy the present. Raking over the memory keeps it alive and poisons today without changing the past.

If we cannot move on by ourselves, we may want to seek outside help. Without moving on, we are cursing our present existence and the existence of those around us.

'What is hell?
Hell is oneself,
Hell is alone, the other figures in it
Merely projections.'

T S Eliot

May 18

Secrets

'And whatsoever I shall see or hear in the course of my profession, as well as outside my profession in my intercourse with men, if it be what should not be published abroad, I will never divulge holding such things to be holy secrets.'

Hippocrates

People tell us things. Whether they tell us they are secrets or not, they have talked to us. They haven't shared it with a room full of people. We want to respect their confidences. We want to keep their secrets for them.

If they want to go and tell others, that is their affair, not ours.

We want to be able to go and discuss our problems with someone, without it becoming a generally known fact. If we are unable to keep the secrets of others, how can we expect anyone to keep our secrets?

If we want the world to know facts about us, we want to be able to choose when and how this happens.

We want to be trusted, and we want to be able to trust others. Then we can get on peacefully with our lives.

'Once the toothpaste is out the tube, it's awfully hard to get it back in.'

Oliver Franks

May 19

Cycles

'O! Swear not by the moon, the inconstant moon, that monthly changes in her circled orb.'

William Shakespeare – Romeo and Juliet

Our moods change. It is easy to notice when we are up, or down, and assume that our feelings will just go on and on.

I have a wise friend, and whenever I tell him I am feeling good, he says "This too shall pass."

He's not being negative. I believe that he says this so that if or when I feel down, I shall remember that 'This too shall pass.' Whereas, if he were to say it only when I felt down, I would be far less likely to believe him.

Just as the moon waxes and wanes, so do we, so does everything.

But whatever happens, it is good to live the moment, to the full, to be present in the world around us. And to help others to enjoy life as much as it is possible.

'Light breaks where no sun shines;
Where no sea runs, the waters of the heart
Push in their tides.'

Dylan Thomas

May 20

Judging

'It is well when judging a friend, to remember that he is judging you with the same godlike and superior impartiality.'

Arnold Bennett

Judging people is a dangerous business. Even if all we do is just assume that they are this or that type of person, it lessens them, and it diminishes us. And if we are making assumptions about them, then they are making them about us.

Much better to be open, looking for the good in people and life. Search out things that we can praise, rather than picking holes in the world about us.

It is delightful to be on the lookout, with a glad heart, for the beauty that surrounds us.

It's so good when we can go out of our way to be delighted.

'I shall tell you a great secret, my friend. Do not wait for the last judgement, it takes place every day.'

Albert Camus

May 21

Spirituality

'Life is real! Life is earnest!
And the grave is not its goal.
Dust thou art, to dust returnest,
Was not spoken of the soul.'

H W Longfellow

We arrive on earth as spirits or souls in a human body. Our souls need us to experience the world so that they can grow.

To be human is to be imperfect, and it is good to accept our imperfections, our faults, our wrongdoings and then move on from them. To take them as necessary evils, through which we must travel.

We learn by experimenting and experiencing both the good and the bad. We learn by making mistakes. If we think that we do not make mistakes – that is a mistake.

Our challenge is to move on, and neither repeat nor dwell on them. And to learn to enjoy living a radiant life. Even if you can only achieve one second of radiance a day, that is a whole second that you didn't have before, which is over six minutes of radiance a year. And surely anyone can achieve a second a day.

'No coward soul is mine,
No trembler in the world's storm-troubled sphere;
I see Heaven's glories shine,
And Faith shines equal, arming me from Fear.'

Emily Brontë

May 22

Freedom

'If there are no dogs in Heaven, then when I die I want to go to where they went.'

Will Rogers

Three stories about dogs!

[Beware one is very sad, you can decide which it is.]

A friend of mine was hunting with his dog, and the dog fell off a cliff. My friend finally managed to climb down and he found Rusty lying with his back broken. They shared their love for each other, and then my friend put his gun to Rusty's head and shot him.

I was walking my puppy Treacle in a wood. She was in the habit of running off for 10-15 minutes before returning happily. It was stressful while I called and waited. This time she did not return. I called and called. After half an hour of calling and hunting for her. I saw a leaf tremble. I went over, and there was Treacle, sinking in a bog, trembling but totally silent. She would, I believe, have stayed silent until she sank or starved to death. I pulled her free.

There is a woman who walks her dog, called (by me) shoebox dog because she had found the dog on the side of the motorway in a shoebox. She always has her dog on one of those extending leads. One day I asked her "Why don't you ever let her off the lead?" to which she replied, "I am frightened she would run off, and I would never see her again".

'All his life, he tried to be a good person. Many times, however, he failed. For, after all, he was only human. He wasn't a dog.'

Charles M Schulz

May 23rd

There
are
no
rules

It is possible to **do** things

However
you
want
!

May 24

Awareness

'The first and wisest of them all professed
To know this only, that he nothing knew.'

John Milton

Once we think we know something, it's easy to close our minds to it. We cease to explore it, our awareness of it diminishes, our world shrinks.

Whether it's something we do or things we look at, listen to, touch, taste or smell, the moment we believe we know them, they lose their gloss.

We may always do something the same way, and it may be a good way, but if other people do it differently, it's worth considering that there might be a better way.

Once we label an object, or own it, or believe that we know it, we stop looking at it. We just see the picture we've already stored in our database.

Take a moment and look at, taste, be present in your world.

If we can develop the habit of experiencing the world as a new place, as the adventure it is, we switch on the light in our lives.

'Three wise men – Are you serious?'

Graffiti

May 25

Goals

'I was seized by the stern hand of Compulsion, that dark unseasonable Urge that impels women to clean house in the middle of the night.'

James Thurber

It could be called the 'Headless Chicken Syndrome', we dash around doing things that must be done, without any clear idea of how the end result will be achieved.

We all have dreams, things we would like to do, but in all honesty, most of them never happen because they just waft around in our heads.

In 1950 they asked all the Harvard graduates "Do you have goals? Are they written down? Do you have a plan for achieving them?"

3% said "Yes."

Interviewed again, in 1970, the net worth of the 3% was higher than the net worth of the 97%. There is more to life than money, but success is nearly always rewarded financially.

To convert our dreams into reality, we want to write them down and create a plan to achieve them. And we want to review them regularly to see how we are getting on.

Then we can succeed.

'But men must know, that in the theatre of man's life it is reserved only for God and angels to be lookers-on.'

Francis Bacon

May 26

Pain

'The least pain in our little finger gives us more concern and uneasiness than the destruction of millions of our fellow beings.'

William Hazlitt

Pain is a gateway to our soul. Rather than fighting it, it's good if we take a few moments of meditation to go into it. If we go into the blackness of our pain absolutely, we can enter the stillness and the wonder of our soul.

At the centre of the pain, there is a pinprick, a mustard seed of pure brilliant white light, which is our being, our soul, this is Universal Unconditional Love and Healing.

It is within us always. We don't need to be experiencing pain to find it. But we can use the pain to focus our mind if we choose to.

When we go into it, we change the pain. We change ourselves.

Whenever we find the light, we can let it grow, fill us, radiate out of us, so that we become brilliant white radiating beings.

'He who knows others is wise;
He who knows himself is enlightened.'

Lao Tzu

May 27

Chance

'Luck affects everything. Let your hook always be cast. In the stream where you least expect it, there will be a fish.'

Ovid

If we are lucky, we may have more than one chance of seizing opportunities. But when they come, they come shrouded in fear, because we can never see where they lead.

The unknown is scary, but the alternative, if we realised it, is scarier still, the risk of the everlasting regret of what might have been.

Take chances when they come. Have adventures. Live.

'In the long run, in spite of everything, I have been lucky. I asked for bread and was given a stone. It turned out to be precious.'

Quentin Crisp

May 28

Dependency

'The greatest day in your life and mine is when we take total responsibility for our attitudes. That's the day we truly grow up.'

John C Maxwell

If our emotional well-being or happiness is dependent on people or things, then they have control of us.

If we can only be happy/contented/balanced as long as 'they' love us, do what we want, or want to be with us, then we have lost our ability to live freely. We have also put our emotional fetters on them.

We can love or be happy with other people, but emotional freedom and maturity come when we enjoy life, because we are living it, not because 'they' are in it.

If our happiness is dependent on people, places and things, our partner, our car, our house, etc. we want to take a serious look at ourselves and our priorities.

'When you have confidence, you can have a lot of fun. And when you have fun, you can do amazing things'

Joe Namath

May 29

Love

'Love seeketh not itself to please,
Nor for itself hath any care:
But for another gives its ease,
And builds a Heaven in Hell's despair.'

William Blake

We all want to be loved. We all need to be loved. Some of us more than others.

Many people find it difficult to love others or to allow others to love them. They think about their lives, their failures, and mistakes, and find it impossible to forgive themselves or accept that others could forgive them.

We all make mistakes, and if we can choose to accept them and forgive ourselves, we can move on from them. Without our failures, we would be far less, and if we can use our experiences as a foundation, we can start to realise that we have value.

If we have something that we can give to others, and we can offer it with love, we no longer need to view ourselves as wicked and useless.

When we accept and love ourselves, we can love others. And in doing that, we open the door which enables us to receive love from others.

'All, everything that I understand, I understand only because I love. Everything is, everything exists, only because I love. Everything is united by it alone. Love is God, and to die means that I, a particle of love, shall return to the general and eternal source.

Leo Tolstoy

May 30

Time

'In the playground of my imagination.'

John Cooper Clarke

It is incredible what one can do with one's mind.

Think, if you will, of something that you are going to do in the not too distant future.

A nice thing would be good if by chance you have one. (I do hope you do.)

Now imagine that it is going to happen in a couple of hours. Move it in your mind to the place where you keep things that are going to happen in two hours.

Now think about something completely different – the colour of your front door, for instance.

Now think about the event again and realise that you imagine and feel that it is going to happen in two hours.

There you are, you no longer need to wait in misery for things, move them so that they are happening soon and enjoy the feeling of excited anticipation that goes with it.

'The distinction between past, present and future is only a stubbornly persistent illusion.'

Albert Einstein

'Time is an illusion. Lunchtime doubly so.'

Douglas Adams

May 31

Oneness

'The only path wide enough for us all is love.'

Kamand Kojouri

'I am here just to honour your beauty, love, and life. We are the reflection of each other. We are one.'

Debasish Mridha

We are one
We love each other.
We have been together since time began.
Sometimes we forget and feel sadness, loneliness or blackness, but we only need to remember that we are one, to be whole again.
We are one.
Filled with love, peace and joy.
We are one.

'We are one, after all, you and I, together we suffer, together exist and forever will recreate each other.'

Pierre Teilhard de Chardin

'When there is no enemy within, the enemies outside cannot hurt you.'

Winston Churchill

Enjoy

June 1

Love

'Birth, and copulation, and death.
That's all the facts when you come to brass tacks:
Birth, and copulation, and death.
I've been born, and once is enough.'

T S Eliot

Surely there's more to life than that?

We've all seen films, read books, where people waste their lives. And sometimes, maybe, we think we don't want to waste our lives. We want to change, to be present in our lives and in the lives of those we love. And then tomorrow comes, and nothing's changed.

If only we could. If only we would. If only.

And yet it is possible to change the way we exist.

~~~

'I want to do with you what spring does with the cherry trees'

Pablo Neruda

Why don't we? Why not make the decision, this once, to change, forever? To be here. To be present. To hug and care for, and to love and laugh.

Wouldn't that be WOW! Wouldn't that be worth waking up for? Everyday.

'I had made a decision to live everyday not as if it were my last day, but as if it were my only day; not so that I would remember it in a year or even a month, but so that at the end of it, when I lay down at night, I could say that I had not wasted it, not sleepwalked through it, that I had lived it.'

Peter Ferry
~~~

June 2

Beliefs

'There is nothing that can help you understand your beliefs better than trying to explain them to an inquisitive child.'

Frank Clark

What do we believe about the world, about how things work, about ourselves?

Between the ages of 16 to 24, everything is very black and white. We know what we believe, and we know it's true, there can be no question about it, and anyone who disagrees is an ignorant idiot.

Hopefully, as we grow older, we will realise that things may not be as entirely set in stone as we thought. Until we realise that the more, we know, the less we know.

However, even then we have beliefs that we hold very firmly, especially about the kind of people we are, and also based on things we 'don't like' and have written off.

The joy of experimenting, exploring experiences with an open mind, will add wonder to our lives if we dare.

It is as if we have been in the same room all our lives and believed 'this is it'. Then a young, energetic, lively, beautiful person appears, flips open a panel and switches on a mass of lights and transforms the room.

Our only challenge is to allow anyone into our room.

Take the risk. Explore the world. We are only here once. Don't let's waste our chance.

'The man who believes in giraffes would swallow anything.'

Adrian Mitchell

June 3

Self Esteem

'He was a self-made man who owed his lack of success to nobody.'

Joseph Heller

Sometimes we feel less than good, and quite naturally, we react. The reaction may manifest itself in a vast number of ways, anger, attention-seeking, frustration, impatience, people-pleasing, depression, wanting to buy things we don't need, dishonesty, isolation, a constant desire to feel different, and feeling sorry for ourselves.

All or any of these probably stem back to a lack of self-worth, self-esteem.

Realising this and identifying the cause of our behaviour is a start. It is the first steppingstone to being able to change it. The next step is to perceive that we are worthy, and we are okay. Troubles come from our vain attempts to steer our lives with a broken rudder.

If we can begin to go inside and listen to our inner voice, guidance, we can start to relax.

If we let the light into our lives and look for ways that we can do things with and for others, rather than trying to curl up and hide inside ourselves, we may accept ourselves.

'No man is an island, entire of itself; every man is a piece of the continent, a part of the main.'

John Donne

'No one can make you feel inferior, without your consent.'

Eleanor Roosevelt

June 4

Awareness

'Normally, we do not so much look at things, as overlook them.'

Alan Watts

Have you ever bought a new pair of shoes, and left the shop wearing them, with the thought as you look at the old shoes 'How could I possibly have been wearing something as scruffy as those?'

Maybe, maybe not. Most of us do take things in our life for granted, accepting them as being the way they are. We put on a little weight and do little about it. We say uncharitable things about people, and we don't notice. We let people mock or criticise us without defending ourselves. We talk about the negative things in the world, not the positive.

It's unlikely that we do all of them, but it's probable that we're guilty of several. And we don't notice it happening.

How much better and fulfilling to choose to take control of our lives and decide to make a difference. To no longer accept the second rate, but to do whatever we can to achieve excellence in more areas of our existence.

'You and I do not see things as they are. We see things as we are.'

Herb Cohen

'Each day I live in a glass room
Unless I break it with the thrusting
Of my senses and pass through
The splintered walls to the great landscape.'

Mervyn Peake

June 5

Moving on

'It is this ability to bear what is unbearable and go on living, to go on doing what one is used to doing – it is this uncanny ability that the existence of the human race is based on.'

Christa Wolf

Do something for me – please...

Think back a year or more to what has happened to you during your life and see if you can find five things that are a constant source of pain and distress for you.

[Most people can only think of a couple – and they have (generally) come to terms with them.]

Now if you would – please... (assuming that you've done the above.)

Think of the things that are troubling/distressing you in the present – your troubles, the things that are keeping you awake at night, upsetting your peace of mind.

And now, take a moment and realise that by comparison to the past, your present troubles, are really nothing.

And now – surely – choose peace of mind.

'Below my window... The blossom is out in full now... I see it is the whitest, frothiest, blossomiest blossom that there ever could be, and I can see it. Things are both more trivial than they ever were, and more important than they ever were, and the difference between the trivial and the important doesn't seem to matter. But the nowness of everything is absolutely wondrous.'

Dennis Potter (on his heightened awareness of things, in the face of his imminent death.)

June 6

Expectations

'now and then
there is a person born
who is so unlucky
that he runs into accidents
which started to happen
to somebody else.'

Don Marquis

Some people say, 'Why does this always happen to me?' It's possible that, from time to time, we may ask the question ourselves. There are times when it almost appears that the world is conspiring to bring us down.

One of the truths about this is, if it's frequently happening to us, it is because we are putting ourselves in a place/situation where it can happen.

It may seem extraordinary that we would choose to do this to ourselves. Surely, we would realise that if we do 'this', with 'them', 'there' then we will get 'X'. And yet often we simply fail to make the connections. Also, no doubt, we feel secure about doing 'this' with 'them' etc., because it is familiar, and we like familiarity.

So if an 'X' that we don't want is happening, maybe it is time to take a serious look at ourselves and our choices.

'We had the experience but missed the meaning.'

T S Eliot

'I learned... that one can never go back, that one should not ever try to go back – that the essence of life is going forward. Life is really a One-Way Street.

Agatha Christie

June 7

Change

'All conservatism is based upon the idea that if you leave things alone, you leave them as they are. But you do not. If you leave a thing alone, you leave it to a torrent of change.'

G K Chesterton

'And now for something completely different.'

Monty Python

We change We are changing We have changed.

We don't remember how we were. (We may have vague memories, but once we move on, we start to forget)

We are becoming who we will be, next week, next year.

We can influence what we become. What we put in is what we will get out, if we sow negative seeds and expectations, that's what we will get.

If we want to be happier, more outgoing, positive, with more vibrant, fuller lives, start sowing the seeds.

Find the positive in whatever is happening to us now and focus on that.

It may be raining, but you can be grateful you're alive. Choose your attitude.

'The butterfly often forgets that it was once a caterpillar.'

Proverb

'Toto, I've a feeling we're not in Kansas anymore.'

Judy Garland

June 8

Revenge

'For we do not expect evil of those we love the most.'

Peter Abelard

She bought her house.
She paid her mortgage.
She came home and found her boyfriend with a girl, who was not only in her bed but also wearing her T-shirt.
So what did she do?
What would you do?
Knot your stomach.
Flash with hatred and revenge?
And then?
And then – well – move on of course.
The alternatives are so much worse than moving on.
The alternatives are **all so much worse** than moving on.
Let us have peace.

'If you seek revenge, you should dig two graves.'

Confucius

'The past is a foreign country; they do things differently there.'

L P Hartley

'Don't go into Mr McGregor's garden: your father had an accident there, he was put into a pie by Mrs. McGregor.

Beatrix Potter – from "Peter Rabbit"

June 9

Growth

'To dry one's eyes and laugh at a fall,
And, baffled, get up and begin again.'

Robert Browning

It is not how many times we get knocked down that matters. It is how many times we get up.

Things go wrong, we experience pain, and then growth, and finally tranquility. All of life is a series of these events.

But we're human, we forget. It is too easy to wallow in each difficulty we experience and be overwhelmed. We become buried in the struggle, the enormity of it all, blind to everything except the current tragedy.

(You may believe that you are not as bad as that. But our unconscious hides our previous pain, lest life becomes unbearable.)

If only we could remember that we have already walked through the snow, and left a track, and now we can follow in our footsteps, and make the journey easier.

All of life is a series of trials and triumphs. To triumph, we have to go through the trials.

Accepting that, remembering it, embracing it, is, in fact, one of the trials we have to go through.

'If the creator had a purpose in equipping us with a neck, he surely meant us to stick it out.'

Arthur Koestler

June 10

Fear or Love

'The only thing we have to fear is fear itself.'

Franklin D Roosevelt

Everything is either love or fear.

So, all our negative feelings – irritation, sarcasm, disrespect, anger, despair, sloth, hatred, greed (please feel free to continue the list) are fear.

When I was finally able to grasp this, I discovered that when I had a negative emotion, I no longer needed to go into it, to expand it, I simply had to think, 'Oh that's fear' and move from the fear to love. It is one of the most liberating discoveries I've ever made. And no, I don't always achieve it, but every time I do, I get better at it.

So, everything is fear or love. And you can go into your body now and find, with a gentle smile, love.

And then with just the tiniest amount of practice, you can move your negative feelings, your fear, into love and bathe in the joy that goes with that.

Of course, we will continue to experience fear. But the more we step from fear to love, the easier it becomes, and the better we feel.

'There is no fear in love, but perfect love casteth out fear.'

John I ch 4 v 18

'To fear love is to fear life, and those who fear life are already three parts dead.'

Bertrand Russell

June 11

Problems

'I never complained at the vicissitudes of fortune, nor murmured at the ordinances of Heaven, excepting once, when my feet were bare, and I had not the means of procuring myself shoes. I entered the great the mosque at Cufah with a heavy heart when I beheld a man who had no feet. I offered up praise and thanksgiving to God for his bounty, and bore with patience the want of shoes.'

Sadi

It's hard, at times, to believe that there are people whose troubles are more significant than ours.

And when we don't have any troubles 'today' it's hard to remember those of our past or to imagine new ones in the future.

But nothing is flat, life goes up and down, and little inconveniences we experience may equate to the mountains other people have to overcome.

Whether mountains or molehills challenge us, we can use either to strengthen us and enable us to be better people in the future, if we choose to be.

'Every problem is a gift – without problems we would not grow.'

Tony Robbins

'Mishaps are like knives, that either serve us or cut us, as we grasp them by the blade or the handle.'

James Russell Lowell

June 12

Change

'Fain I would climb, yet fear I to fall.'

Sir Walter Raleigh

[Written on a windowpane. Queen Elizabeth wrote below it]

'If thy heart fails thee, climb not at all.'

Queen Elizabeth I

It is not easy to dare – to change.

As soon as we consider it, we tend to run mental movies of possible outcomes. And often there are more negative outcomes than positive ones, especially if we have tried and failed in the past.

If we go inside, into the now, which is meditating, we can let all the negatives drop away. For in the now, in this moment, fear, guilt, projections do not exist.

When we reach now, we can use it to think about what we want to achieve. We can decide the next thing that we want to do, to move towards our goal.

It is possible – and good – when we return from our inner journey, to leave part of us in a state of meditation. In this way, as we go through the day, we will be in touch with the strength that comes from our inner self.

'There must be a beginning of any great matter, but the continuing, unto the end until it be thoroughly finished yields the true glory.'

Francis Drake

'To live is to change, and to be perfect is to have changed often.'

John Henry Newman

June 13

Responsibility

'Where he falls short, 'tis Nature's fault alone;
Where he succeeds, the merit's all his own.'

Charles Churchill

It is so easy to blame anything – the world, nature, other people, the government, our parents, the weather, our big toe – for anything that goes wrong in our lives, while feeling smugly self-satisfied for all our triumphs and our minor achievements.

The truth is that we are responsible for what occurs to us. We are continually moving along, steering our ship, both when we are becalmed and when tossed around by a storm.

Accepting responsibility, realising that it is our hand on the wheel that guides us, empowers us, enables us to choose what course to take, and to accept the present.

When we accept this, without blame or recrimination, we can make the best of our experience and our lives.

'Accuse not nature, she hath done her part;
Do thou but thine.'

John Milton

June 14

Communication

‘ “Then you should say what you mean,” the March Hare went on. “I do,” Alice hastily replied, “at least – at least I mean what I say – that’s the same thing you know.” “Not the same thing a bit!” said the Hatter. “Why, you might just as well say that ‘I see what I eat’ is the same thing as ‘I eat what I see.” ’

Lewis Carroll

Quite often, people fail to say what they mean. Quite often we fail to understand what they’re saying, – even when we listen to it.

In all honesty, a lot of the time, this doesn’t matter, we’re not engaged in meaningful exchanges, we’re just making appropriate noises to one another.

There are moments when it does matter. And when they happen, we want to shut up and listen. (Which is extremely hard for some of us.) And only after we have genuinely listened, and clarified what we have heard, do we then want to make our contribution.

It’s too easy to dive in, give our opinions on the first thing we hear, when in fact, that is not what is being said at all.

‘Mike: There’s no word in the Irish language for what you were doing.
Wilson: In Lapland, they have no word for snow.’

Joe Orton

June 15

Advice

'Get the advice of everybody whose advice is worth having – they are very few – and then do what you think best yourself.

Charles Stewart Parnell

People come to us with their problems, and we often know precisely what they should do, and we tell them.

(Sometimes we think "I'm glad I'm not in his situation because I wouldn't want to do what I've just told him to do.")

And yet if/when we are in the same situation ourselves, we have no idea what to do, because we cannot look at ourselves objectively.

(I think that, sometimes/often, God sends us people who have the same problems as us, so that if we were really smart, we could listen to our advice and do it.)

Leaving that aside, when we have problems/challenges, it's sensible to seek advice, so that somebody who isn't suffering from the problem, can give us an unbiased view.

Then we will undoubtedly do what we want to do, possibly, guided by their suggestions.

'Pooh began to feel a little more comfortable, because when you are a Bear of Very Little Brain, and you Think of Things, you find sometimes that a Thing which seemed very Thingish inside you is quite different when it gets out into the open and has other people looking at it.'

A A Milne

June 16

Success

'Success makes life easier. It doesn't make living easier.'

Bruce Springsteen

Real success and ambition aren't keeping up with, or overtaking the Joneses, the new car, bigger house, more money than we can use. It isn't doing things so that people can look at us with awe.

True, honest, deep down inside us, success is learning to live in peace.

If we can accept others as they are, and also accept ourselves, without the need for recognition from others, we can have peace and joy.

When we take our focus away from ourselves and the things 'we want' and instead go into the world with 'what can I do for you' as our goal, then we will achieve something.

Life's a journey. On journeys, we do the same small things over and over. But each moment is a new event, a unique opportunity, a new choice, and we can live a far more fulfilling life when we remember that.

No one succeeds all the time. But some of us can succeed some of the time. And when we do it makes it all worthwhile.

'At the end of your life you will never regret not having passed one more test, not winning one more verdict or not closing one more deal. You will regret time not spent with a husband, a friend, a child or a parent.'

Barbara Bush

June 17

Anger

'Go directly – see what she's doing and tell her she mustn't!'

Punch

Anger! What a killer. How debilitating. What an incredible drain of our energies.

Whether at home, in a queue, in the car, at work, how easy it is to let impatience and anger seep into our minds and bodies, like a poison.

Maybe it doesn't seep, perhaps it floods.

Why? Why do we let it consume us?

If we were to step back for a moment and look dispassionately at the situation, as an angel might, a non-judgmental third party, his wings and arms folded, a slight smile on his face. He watches, as we stand, red-faced, with steam leaking out of our ears and poison dribbling into our brain, while in front of us in the queue, a young couple, totally happy and oblivious, are just getting on with their lives.

Or take another more sinister scene at home or work. We, enveloped in our own steam and poison, they frightened, damaged by our anger, poison squirting into their lives too, as they struggle 'to do their best' – something which, in our eyes, they will never achieve.

What kind of person would choose to live with impatience and anger, when they could decide to enjoy the world and have the world delight in them?

'It is stupidity second to none, to busy oneself with the correction of the world.'

Moliere

June 18

Arguments

'There's a hole in my bucket, dear Liza, dear Liza.'

Nursery Rhyme

Even a pinprick in a bucket allows the water to seep away.

Arguments, however small, do the same to our energy. I am not saying that we shouldn't have heated debates with others, that can empower us.

But arguments, all the way from the 'Let's fight over this' down to the petty 'I wish you would put the salt back where it belongs', all drain us. Disempower us.

And both they and we are adding fuel to flames.

If when we realise this is happening, we stop and withdraw from the issue, it nearly always ends.

It's no fun fighting when there's nothing to hit.

'I am not arguing with you, I am telling you.'

James McNeill Whistler

' "For your own good" is a persuasive argument that will eventually make a man agree to his own destruction.'

Janet Frame

June 19

Complaints

'One of the depressing things about depression is knowing that there are lots of people in the world with far more reason to feel depressed than you have, and finding that, far from making you snap out of your depression, it only makes you despise yourself more and thus feel more depressed.'

David Lodge

We don't need to reach depression to be suffering. Some people just moan and complain their way through the day.

They drag themselves and all about them down too.

If we participate in their moans or let them get away with them, we are merely perpetuating their state.

If we refuse to talk to them when they complain, if we change the subject, tell them we're not going to play that game anymore, it can be the start of a change.

(If we are the moaners – God helps those who helps themselves.)

'Mirth is like a flash of lightning that breaks through a gloom of clouds and glitters for a moment; cheerfulness keeps up a kind of daylight in the mind and fills it with a steady and perpetual serenity.'

Bertrand Russell

June 20

Giving

'You have not lived today until you have done something for someone who can never repay you.'

John Bunyan

Do things for others without expectation.

Challenge yourself to do something for somebody today, and not get found out.

Look for ways to improve the lives of others. The light that fills you as you do selfless deeds is enough reward.

And yet there is more.

When you cast your bread upon the waters – it comes back sandwiches.

The rewards don't necessarily come from the recipients of your generosity and selfless love.

The rewards come from unexpected places. And they will enrich your life beyond your imagination.

'When I give, I give myself.'

Walt Whitman

June 21

Positive Talk

'That "Mummy – watch – me – jump" need to impress.'

Nigella Lawson

'Be careful! Don't fall off the wall!'

What do they do? They fall off the wall, of course. They hadn't even been considering falling. But along we came and put the idea in their head. Their unconscious hears it and thinks 'Oh I know how to do that, I'm good at that' and bang down they come.

Even when we have grown out of walking on walls, we are warned about 'not doing', about failure, about all the pitfalls that could lie ahead. Unsurprisingly this leads either to failure or worse still, not starting at all.

Our words want to be positive rather than negative, and then the rate of success will dramatically increase.

Instead of 'Don't fall off the wall' how about, 'Wow! You're so good at balancing'. Rather than 'Most people who do that fail' how about, 'To succeed takes dedication and I know that's something you've always found easy to do'.

'Man needs difficulties; they are necessary for health.'

Carl Jung

June 22

Adventure

'Thanks to the Interstate Highway System, it is now possible to travel across the country from coast to coast without seeing anything.'

Charles Kuralt

'When you set out for Ithaka
Ask that your way be long.'

Constantine Cavafy

What kind of a traveler through life are you? When I started this morning I had it in mind to write about difficulties, but I couldn't find a quote that served me, so I followed the path through such things as disaster and disillusion and finally found my way to travel. A joyous journey it was.

As I drive around the country and I pass a road that calls to me, I wonder where it goes, and I explore it to find out.

When I read, I look up the meanings of words I don't know. You might describe me as an adventurer. My life is full of fun. And why not, there isn't time to sit around waiting to die. Let others do that.

'As for disappointing them, I should not so much mind; but I can't abide to disappoint myself.'

Oliver Goldsmith

June 23

Acceptance

'Men will always be mad, and those who think they can cure them are the maddest of all.'

Voltaire

'Madness need not be all breakdown. It may also be break-through.'

R D Laing

So we are all mad. Well, that's a relief. That means that there's something wrong with everybody – Not just me.

Or, I'm not the only one who feels different – everyone else does too – whether they admit it or not. (And of course, they won't.) So it's okay to be different and to feel different.

What fun! That means I can be me.

And so, unfettered I can go forth and develop. The sky can be my oyster, or a bowling ball can be my balloon.

There ain't no limits now.

But most importantly, it means we no longer want to judge others or ourselves, and we can embrace the world with joyful acceptance.

'In one and the same fire, clay grows hard and wax melts.

Francis Bacon

'The mind of man is capable of anything.'

Joseph Conrad

June 24

God

'That deeply emotional conviction of the presence of a superior reasoning power, which is revealed in the incomprehensible universe, forms my idea of God.'

Albert Einstein

'God has no religion.'

Mahatma Gandhi

Whether we follow, believe, or rejoice in one of the many religions, and their Gods or not, most of us have an idea that there is a Power Greater than ourselves, which for simplicity's sake we'll refer to as God.

We can search for God in nature, in prayer and meditation, church services, retreats, or pilgrimage. Or we may just muddle along not considering God at all. However, at times of death and stress most of us turn our minds to God. The concept of God lies within all of us.

We do not need to 'do' anything. We only need to go inside ourselves to find that power that is greater than we are, to find the guide and strength that we require, to move towards spiritual wholeness. We are all one – with God.

' "God is, or he is not." But to which side shall we incline?... Let us weigh the gain and loss in wagering that God is. Let us estimate the two chances. If you gain, you gain all; if you lose, you lose nothing. Wager then without hesitation that he is.'

Blaise Pascal

'God don't come when you want Him, but He's right on time.'

Anon

June 25

Participation

'Each man's death diminishes me,
For I am involved in Mankind.
Therefore, send not to know
For whom the bell tolls,
It tolls for thee.

John Donne

It is so easy to forget our interdependence on, and our connectivity to, those around us and the world.

Everything we do creates ripples. In a Roald Dahl short story about fighter pilots in the last war, when the siren sounded for take-off, they counted to 20, before boarding their planes – so that they would not be there when the enemy shot at them.

If we don't go to the supermarket, somebody else will take our place at the checkout. If we hadn't gone out with 'X' and married them, they would probably have found someone else.

So the decisions we make today do not just affect us.

There are times when we do not want to do things but doing them will make a difference. There are also times when we want to do something, and yet we know we should not. Whatever we do – we create ripples –we are responsible.

'We're all in this together by ourselves.'

Lily Tomlin

June 26

Kindness

'That best portion of a good man's life,
His little, nameless, unremembered acts
Of kindness and of love.'

William Wordsworth

The difference between doing something kind and unkind is often very slight.

An act or a word of unkindness can wound, scar, and be carried forward by the giver or the receiver. If we think back with a shudder to some small meanness that we said or performed, it may trouble us for the rest of our lives, as may a thoughtless lie.

We don't want to put down markers in our lives, that we can look back at and regret.

Nor do we want others to carry the memory of some criticism or cruelty that we created.

Quite apart from any damage we may do to others, how comfortable to be able to lay our heads upon the pillow at night, aware that we have not only done acts of kindness throughout the day but avoided acts of unkindness too.

'Three things in human life are important. The first is to be kind. The second is to be kind. The third is to be kind.'

Henry James

'Be kind, for everyone you meet is fighting a hard battle.'

Plato

June 27

Stupidity

'I am more stupid about some things than about others; not equally stupid in all directions; I am not a well-rounded person.'

Saul Bellow

It is difficult to contemplate, let alone admit that we may not know as much as... that we might not be as wise... as smart as we often...

There are times when we know we don't know something. There might even be times when we realise that the thing we're doing, or that some of the things we've done are not as brilliant as we thought. If we think about them at all, that is.

Obviously, the reason that the country's in the mess it's in is because it's not run by celebrities, keyboard warriors, and armchair managers.

Leaving the country aside for a moment, perhaps we could improve the quality of our lives and of those about us by considering our beliefs, attitudes and behaviours.

'A fool sees not the same tree that a wise man sees.'

William Blake

'How come the things that happen to stupid people, happen to me?'

Homer Simpson

June 28

Confidence

'As I was walking up the stair,
I met a man who wasn't there
He wasn't there again today,
Oh how I wish he'd go away.'

Hugh Mearns

Don't be the person nobody notices, the person who's name nobody can remember. I once asked a friend how he managed to be so confident. He is the sort of person who walks into a room full of strangers, and within no time there's a group around him, laughing and talking.

'I'm not confident' he told me 'I'm really shy too.'

He had taught himself to talk to people, to ask them questions, to engage them. And I guess, he'd learnt that everybody's shy, but also, and more importantly, that if you make an effort with people, they'll make an effort back.

If you have trouble with this, practice. Practice wherever you go. Talk to the people at the checkouts, get the cashier to smile.

If you are in a social or business setting, stick your hand out and say 'I'm...' Ask them questions, be interested in them. Have fun, challenge yourself.

'Fate chooses our relations, we choose our friends.'

Jacques Delille

June 29

Knowledge

'So that means you need to know things even when you don't need to know them. You need to know them not because you need to know them but because you need to know whether or not you need to know. And if you don't need to know you still need to know so that you know that there was no need to know.'

Jonathan Lynn and Antony Jay

Some people suffer from the need to have opinions about everything. Some people suffer from the fact that they believe that their views are the only right ones.

Even if we are not as extreme as that, there is a tendency to embrace information that supports our ideas, and to reject other people's thoughts and beliefs, when they don't conform with ours.

It is easy to let life flow past, without even considering what our ideas and beliefs are because nothing ever questions them.

Perhaps it is good to take a few moments to stop and look and consider and even wonder at what it is that is creating our reality.

'In his brain –
Which is as dry as the remainder biscuit
After a voyage – he hath strange places crammed
With observation, the Which he vents
In mangled forms.'

William Shakespeare – As You Like It

June 30

Connectedness

'You are never alone. You are eternally connected with everyone.'

Amit Ray

'The universe and I exist together, and all things are one.'

Chuang Tzu

Whenever anyone we know is going to the sea, we ask, "Throw a stone into the sea for us."

We are all connected by the love that sweeps the world.

Sometimes, some of us, forget about the love, and we march to the madness that the fear in others creates.

We can choose to stop doing that. We can grasp, hold and cherish the love that bonds us.

Throw a stone into the sea for us and for the love that cries out for your embrace.

'They both listened silently to the water, which to them was not just water, but the voice of Life, the voice of Being, the voice of perpetual Becoming.'

Hermann Hesse

July 1

Decisiveness

'Never trust a man who, when left alone in a room with a tea-cosey, doesn't try it on.'

Billy Connolly

So much easier to sit in the room and do nothing. To not even consider the tea-cosey.

Halfway through a play, someone announced that a bomb had been planted in the theatre. Only one member of the audience and one actress ran from the building. They survived.

The people who survive shipwrecks are those who start to act as soon as something goes wrong.

It's easier to go into a dark room when we know what's in there. It makes sense to know how to get out of a building if there's a fire. (That's why there are fire drills.)

If when you arrive at a new place, you explore the fire escapes, are you idiotic and paranoid, or sensible and sane?

We can go through our lives, prepared and decisive, or we can drift along as flotsam at the mercy of the waves.

'The world can only be grasped by action, not by contemplation.... The hand is the cutting edge of the mind.'

Jacob Bronowski / Diane Arbus

July 2

Acceptance

'I always wanted to be somebody. Now I see I should have been more specific.'

Jane Wagner

For the most part, things do not turn out how we want or expect. They are sometimes better, sometimes worse, sometimes nonexistent.

While it is good to make plans and do whatever we can to achieve them, it is also good to accept that things are the way they are.

If we were to take one instrument from an orchestra, a minor one, and play the parts it has in a symphony, it would almost certainly sound somewhat random. But when we add the other instruments, we realise that it is an essential and intrinsic part of the whole.

We cannot honestly know or understand our part in the whole if we are just looking at our immediate lives. We need to trust and believe that the outcome will be the one that is meant. What is important is that we play our part as well as we can, the difficult times are as important as the wonderful ones.

'And my parents finally realise I'm kidnapped, and they snap into action immediately: they rent out my room.'

Woody Allen

July 3

Action

'The truth of the matter is that we always know the right thing to do. The hard part is doing it!

Norman Schwarzkopf

Sometimes it's just too much effort. 'Can't be bothered' flits across the mind. 'I deserve a rest.' 'Why me?'

The difference between the person who has a sink full of dirty dishes and the person who has a bright, sparkling kitchen is simple.

The first person walks in and sees the sink full of dirty dishes and thinks, 'Oh god what a horrible mess, I'll do it later – it doesn't matter – there's nobody to see it – it can wait – I'm too busy', and leaves, adding another plate to the sink.

The second person comes into the kitchen and sees the dishes in the sink and visualises a bright, clean, sparkling kitchen. They quickly, efficiently wash up, enjoying their pristine kitchen. It's no effort, and it takes them very little time.

To do the things we find ourselves putting off, all we need to do is see beyond them, go to the good feeling we'll experience when the task is completed, and get started on it.

Enjoy!

'And thou wilt give thyself relief, if thou doest every act of thy life as if it were the last.'

Marcus Aurelius

July 4

Behaviour

'My real opposition is myself.'

Shah of Iran

Our defects – anger, impatience, jealousy, discontent, procrastination, being judgemental – cripple us, because when we are suffering from any form of negativity, it is impossible to be at our best.

However, they all have opposites, and if we choose to, we can pause and identify the opposite. Anger – love, impatience – patience, discontent – contentment, jealousy – love etc.

Defects originate from positives that have become twisted into negatives. So we can use our weaknesses as signposts to behaviours that can lead to harmony. When we are suffering from defects, not only do we suffer, but we drag the world around us down too.

'Conduct is three-fourths of our life and its largest concern.'

Matthew Arnold

July 5

Change

'Do you think that the things people make fools of themselves about are any less real and true than the things they behave sensibly about? They are more true: they are the only things that are true.'

George Bernard Shaw

On the whole, we try so hard to conceal our shortcoming but, by and large to no avail. Mainly because the person we cannot hide them from is ourselves.

That being the case, we are left with two choices, accept ourselves, warts and all, or change.

Often, one of our problems is that we view and judge the world with a different set of rules to the ones we apply to ourselves. We beat ourselves up unduly for our failures, or we sneer at the behaviours of others. Sometimes we do both, like someone looking down on the world as they lie in the gutter alongside the dogshit.

The world is. We are. Accepting ourselves is more comfortable and probably makes us more pleasant to be around. And if you do want to change, change one thing at a time. Do it with love, not with criticism. Focus on the new behaviour, and gradually it will become the new habit.

'We must be the change we wish to see in the world.'

Mahatma Gandhi

July 6

Communication

'Conversation is like playing tennis with a ball made from Krazy Putty that keeps coming back over the net in a different shape.'

David Lodge

There are people that we'd rather not talk to, so with them maybe that's fine.

But even with people that we care about, we are often like ships passing in the night, both hooting so loudly that they cannot hear the other's hoot.

We can easily get caught up in our thoughts, or our own agenda, just waiting for a gap where we can steer the conversation in the direction we want.

Sometimes we may say about people, 'I daren't ask him/her how their day went, he/she'll tell me.' (Are they saying that about us?)

We all want our chance to speak.

Maybe the way to get what we want is to give what we want. If we truly listen and give our undivided attention, we can then ask for our turn to talk.

We may need to discuss with them the importance of listening, so that they are prepared to make the effort, to take the risk of real communication.

'The trouble with her is that she lacks the power of conversation but not the power of speech.'

George Bernard Shaw

July 7

Wonder

'Is it so small a thing
To have enjoyed the sun,
To have lived light in the spring,
To have loved, to have thought, to have done?'

Matthew Arnold

'Life's a pudding full of plums.'

W S Gilbert

The total amazing, unbelievable wonder of life and the world in which we live.

It may not always feel like that, because we let the daily detritus of our existence cloud our view.

Suppose we can just remember to take precious moments to focus on and to bask in the wonder that surrounds us. Breathtaking. Indescribable.

A petal. A floating speck of dust caught in sunlight. A caring hand brushing us with love. The first taste of a sun-drenched tomato. The ability to smile...

What madness stops us from bathing in the wonder of it every day?

What do we need to do to remember to glory in it?

'Life itself, every moment of it, every drop of it, here, this instant, now, in the sun, in Regent's Park, was enough. Too much, indeed.'

Virginia Woolf

July 8

Thoughts

'I have striven not to laugh at human action, not to weep at them, nor to hate them, but to understand them.'

Buruch Spinoza

"Is there anything I can do about it now?"

Our ego is that part of our mind which is dedicated to entertaining us, lying to us, doing whatever it can to prevent us from being in "this" moment, (which is, incidentally, of course, all we ever have.) Our ego constantly creates thoughts, to distract us, and frequently to cause us pain and disquiet.

So, "Is there anything I can do about it now?"

Nearly always what we are thinking about is something that we could – or should – be doing tomorrow or – ought – to have done yesterday, last week or a year ago.

So when that happens, if we have a valuable idea about what we could do tomorrow, write it down – now. And when we think about it again, we can say "I don't need to think about that – I've written it down."

So liberating to do. Beware though, the ego will do its best to prevent you.

'Only the most intelligent and the most stupid do not change.'

Confucius

'In order to have great happiness you have to have great pain and unhappiness – otherwise how would you know when you're happy?'

Leslie Caron

July 9

Choice

'The truth that makes men free is for the most part the truth which men prefer not to hear.'

Herbert Agar

Twin boys, their mother a drug addict, who overdoses and dies when they are five, their father an alcoholic, petty criminal, in and out of jail. An alcoholic grandmother brings them up.

On reaching their forties, one is an alcoholic, sleeping rough, barely surviving. The other is successful, middle management, wife, two kids, a lovely house.

They are interviewed separately and asked why they are leading the kind of life they are.

Both of them reply, 'Given my background and upbringing, what choice did I have?'

'There is no more miserable human being than one in whom nothing is habitual but indecision.'

William James

July 10

Peace

'No stir of air was there,
Not so much life as on a summer's day
Robs not one light seed from the feather'd grass,
But where the dead leaf fell, there did it rest.'

John Keats

We've all lain under a tree and looked up at the light filtering through the leaves. We've all taken a moment to be at one with nature, to be at peace (I hope).

Mostly we are buffeted by the noise and intrusion of life. It is easy to forget that peace exists, or that we ever experienced it.

It is possible, regardless of the clamour around us, to go inside ourselves to remember and relive episodes of peace, and use them to make us impervious to the onslaught we are experiencing.

'And I shall have some peace there, for peace comes dropping slow,
Dropping from the veils of the morning to where the cricket sings.'

W B Yeats

July 11

Fulfilment

'That's not a friend, that's an employer I'm trying out for a few days.'

Thornton Wilder

It seems that the majority of people complain about the work they do. Leaving aside the money, without a job, we cease to connect with the world, and our lives lack meaning.

In a survey in the USA, people who retired and did not take up something new, had a life expectancy of 18 months. In contrast, those who retired and started a new career had a life expectancy of 18 years.

So, work fulfils and nourishes us. Therefore, it surely makes sense to do something that we enjoy – however great the risk of changing.

The more we enjoy what we do, the better our quality of life in every area.

'Absence of occupation is not rest,
A mind quite vacant is a mind distressed.'

William Cowper

July 12

Acceptance

'The best and most beautiful things in the world cannot be seen or even touched, they must be felt with the heart.'

Helen Keller

We are today, who we are, because of what has gone before. We have accumulated wisdom, and we have also done things which make us think less of ourselves. We can use both to guide us today, to become the person we choose to be.

If we allow our mistakes to haunt us, the shame that we feel will prevent us from moving on.

The best way we can make amends for what we have done is by living fully today. By being the person we can be, by behaving responsibly towards others and ourselves.

The new day starts now, and we do not need to wait until tomorrow, any moment can be a new beginning if we choose to let it be one.

'I can't change the direction of the wind, but I can adjust my sails to always reach my destination.'

James Dean

July 13

Serenity

'God grant me the serenity to accept the things I cannot change....'

Reinhold Niebuhr

It can be a trial to even contemplate the things we cannot change.

No doubt if we have serenity before we start, it will make the task simpler.

What are the things that we can do nothing about, that get us down?

Pick one thing in your life that is a source of irritation. Go into it 'NOW.'

Go into it. Feel it.

Accept that you can do nothing about it.

Go into it and **truly** accept that you can do nothing about it. And now let go of it.

Let it go.

The difficulty, for us, is recognising the challenges, and then accepting that we can do nothing about them. Once we have accepted that fact and have learnt (or started) to 'Let Go', the relief is tangible. We no longer need to do battle with or be troubled by them.

And having let go, we can begin to enjoy increased serenity. It is a blessing and a wonderful release.

'Go placidly amid the noise and the haste and remember what peace there may be in silence.'

Max Ehrmann

July 14

Serenity

'God grant me the serenity
To accept the things I cannot change
Courage to change the things I can
And wisdom to know the difference.'

Reinhold Niebuhr

So we've accepted the things we cannot change, now comes the tricky bit, having the courage to change the things we can.

Having the courage to change isn't a one-off, it's an ongoing awareness of our behaviour. Recognising that we have 'misbehaved', or better still being aware, and changing our behaviour before we do it.

We want to keep the light switched on so that we can see what we are doing, what we've done, and then move towards being the best we can be.

And we want to use our wisdom to make sure that we don't label things as 'their fault' so that we 'cannot do anything about them'.

If we start on the basis that nearly everything in our lives is there because we either created it or allowed its creation, then we are in a position to be able to do something about them.

The joy, peace of mind, serenity and feeling of completeness that comes from vigilantly pursuing this is immense.

And now we want to start again.

' What we call the beginning is often the end
And to make an end is to make a beginning.
The end is where we start from.'

T S Eliot

July 15

Emotions

'As you pass from the tender years of youth into harsh and embittered manhood, make sure you take with you on your journey all the human emotions! Don't leave them on the road, for you will not pick them up afterwards!'

Nikolai Gogol.

I hope, I believe, it is possible to rekindle positive emotions. They may be buried beneath a heap of mouldering blankets, but if we peel the covers away – slowly, or even suddenly – we will find a dormant glimmer of emotion waiting to leap out and embrace us.

It is true that the older we get, the more hidden our emotions can become.

Enthusiasm is contagious – start an epidemic. It is easy to keep our thoughts and interests to ourselves, but if we share them, we will find others who have similar interests. If we exchange our sparks both flames will grow.

We are often taught as adults, that we should suppress our emotions, that it is unbecoming for a grown-up to behave in this or that way. These are lies, taught by the tight-lipped community, who weaned on pickles, want everyone else to wrinkle up their noses at any demonstration of unfettered feelings.

Enthusiasm is not contrary to reason. It is reason – on fire.'

Peter Marshall

July 16

Hope

'Despair is the price one pays for setting oneself an impossible aim.'

Graham Greene

'Take hope from the heart of man, and you make him a beast of prey.'

Ouida

However dark it may be, somewhere, if we look, is a flicker of hope. Wherever we are, someone else has overcome more significant troubles than the ones we face.

'But I ain't got no troubles. I'm fine.'

'Bully for you.'

Most of us have things we hope for, things we are striving to achieve. It is good to have hopes for something achievable today so that we don't get beaten back by discouragement. If we are always aiming too high and failing, we may give up.

Hope requires action and dedication and a plan. It requires self-belief and enjoyment. If the fear of failing to achieve what we hope to accomplish is too great, it can prevent us from doing anything. That is why we want to have realistic hopes.

'It's not the despair, Laura, I can stand the despair. It's the hope.'

Michael Frayn

'There comes a time in a man's life when to get where he has to go – if there are no doors or windows – he walks through a wall.'

Bernard Malamud

July 17

Choice

'The least thing upset him on the links. He missed short putts because of the uproar of the butterflies in the adjoining meadows.'

P G Wodehouse

So easy to be distracted. So easy to blame the outside world for our troubles.

And yet, if we honestly look at our situation, we can see that it is we ourselves who choose the way we dance.

Yes, the outside world may impinge, but we can choose our reaction, we can choose to be the masters of our destiny, or we can simply sink, our screams unheard.

'Life is just one damned thing after another.'

Elbert Hubbard

July 18

Happiness

'The fountain of happiness lies within,
If you ever delve, it will ever spring.'

Marcus Aurelius

We have a choice. Sometimes we forget that we have a choice, and we blunder about, hurting ourselves and others. More often we just move mindlessly through life in quiet discontent, adding little or nothing to our lives or the lives of others.

The saying goes that most people die at the age of 25 and spend the next 40 years waiting for their body to catch up. I'm sure this can't apply to you – you wouldn't be reading this if it did.

We can, however, easily slide into 'less happiness' without noticing. Our gratitude crumbles, we thank and praise people less often, we don't make an effort to give or get a smile. We are human, after all.

It is imperative to know that we create in others our feelings and emotions, and they create theirs in us. So if fear, ingratitude, discontent, or anger creep into our thinking, we start on a downward spiral, hand in hand with those around us.

We can, if we're smart, catch ourselves not being happy and decide to change the way we're behaving, even if we don't want to.

We can choose to start creating joy, light, sunshine, laughter in the lives of others, and ourselves.

Then the fountain will open, and happiness can spring out.

'Happiness is the meaning and the purpose of life, the whole aim and end of human existence.'

Aristotle

July 19

Choice

'Bad things are not the worst things that can happen to us. Nothing is the worst thing that can happen to us.'

Richard Bach

Life goes by... and by... we just cannot stop it. So easy to blink, to sigh and to miss it. So easy to notice the things and people that irritate us – they are after all, 'in our faces', continually drawing attention to themselves, in one way or another.

Our life is a constant flow of decisions and choices. Where shall we point our telescope next? Will we be drawn into what we see, or will we flit on to something else?

We cannot spend time on everything or with everybody. If we try to, we become like butter, spread so thinly it cannot be seen or tasted.

We want to choose what we want to do, who we want to be with, and commit ourselves wholeheartedly to living and enjoying our life.

We want to learn to say 'no' and refuse to be dragged into too many things, into the things we don't want to do.

'Everyone is a bore to someone. That is unimportant. The thing to avoid is being a bore to oneself.'

Gerald Brenan

July 20

Praise

'The advantage of doing one's praising for oneself is that one can lay it on so thick and exactly in the right places.'

Samuel Butler

We long for praise. From birth until death it is the food we crave.

In a survey, top business people said that the thing they wanted more than anything else was 'Recognition' in other words 'Praise'.

And so we want to find ways to praise the people in our lives.

Right from the moment when our three-year-old comes running in, a look of joy and excitement on his face, shouting, 'Look, Mummy! I brought the washing in for you!' as he drags in the mud-covered clothes.

Do we say 'Wow! Johnny that's wonderful! Thank you so much!'

No, we scream and rant. So Johnny retreats mentally bruised, and less than he was.

If we were to praise and then explain how to do it, Johnny could retain his enthusiasm.

Praise wants to be specific and enthusiastic.

Saying, 'Thank you' is not praise.

Saying, 'Thanks for the meal' may be better than saying nothing, but it still isn't praise.

Saying, 'Thank you for the meal, you make the best salad' is praise.

Praise.

Frequently.

'Nothing great was ever achieved without enthusiasm.'

Ralph Waldo Emerson

July 21

Forgiveness

'When a deep injury is done to us, we never recover until we forgive.'

Alan Paton

The main barrier to forgiveness is resentment. As long as we keep the fire of our anger stoked, we can never forgive.

Our anger hurts us, not others. As long as we are carrying it and lack forgiveness, we are damaging ourselves. If someone has harmed us, it happened at the moment of their action. And now we are continuing to hurt ourselves by keeping it alive.

Even if we are in no way to blame for what happened, if we can start by asking ourselves (and or God) for forgiveness for what happened, and forgive ourselves, we can open the door which will enable us to forgive them. Until we have forgiven ourselves, we cannot forgive them.

Jimmy breaks a plate. “Mummy, I broke a plate. I'm so sorry.” “Be careful next time.” “Mummy, I'm so sorry,” “That's OK Jimmy, I forgive you.” “Oh, mummy I can't believe I did anything so awful.” “SHUT UP Jimmy! I've forgiven you, now give me a break OK!”

When we've forgiven, or been forgiven, that's it. We don't need to keep forgiving or asking for forgiveness. It's done. Move on. Stop keeping it alive.

'I ain't saying you treated me unkind
You could have done better but I don't mind
You just kinda wasted my precious time
But don't think twice, it's all right!'

Bob Dylan

July 22

Letting go

'Like the dew on the mountain,
Like the foam on the river,
Like the bubble on the fountain,
Thou art gone, and forever.'

Sir Walter Scott

When someone dies, it's right to mourn, to feel sorrow, to bathe in grief.

It is not right to be still doing it, years later. Three and a half weeks is long enough. That can be three weeks and three days, or three weeks and four days. You get to choose.

We feel guilt when someone dies, all the things that we could, should, might have done for, or with them. However, even if we had done all those things, we would just find other things to feel guilty about.

Life moves on, and rather than remembering them with sorrow, we want to remember them with joy, to enjoy the times we spent together.

Share the moment of 'Now' with your departed grandparent, parent, lover, friend. Go and wonder at, delight in, share a sunset, a flower, a cloud, the wind tugging at your coat. Smile, feel the happiness, be grateful and thank them for sharing it with you.

'Thy voice is on the rolling air;
I hear thee where the waters run;
Thou standeth in the rising sun,
And in the setting thou art fair.'

Alfred, Lord Tennyson

July 23

Self-talk

'You know you haven't stopped talking since I came here? You must have been vaccinated with a phonograph needle.'

Groucho Marx

Nearly all of us talk to ourselves, and many of us spend the whole time criticising ourselves and putting ourselves down.

Become aware of what you're saying to yourself internally, and ask yourself, 'If anyone else talked to me like that, would I keep them as a friend?' 'No!'

Some people may find it easier to ask themselves if I talked to someone else like that, would that person go on spending time with me? 'No!'

Now ask your inner voice if it's trying to help you. It will say, 'Yes.'

Then ask it if what it's currently doing is working. It will say, 'No.'

Ask it if it will do something which will be supportive and helpful, and that will enable it to achieve what it wants for you. 'Yes.'

Now choose a voice that you find encouraging and supportive. Ask your inner voice to speak with that voice. It will.

Next ask it to change what it says, from being critical to being encouraging and supportive. It will do this too.

If the old critical voice returns, remind it that you don't use that voice anymore, you used to use it, but now you use the supportive voice. Enjoy the change.

'They never taste who always drink;
They always talk who never think.'

Matthew Prior

July 24

Imagine

'Imagine there's no countries
It isn't hard to do,
Nothing to kill or die for
And no religion too.'

John Lennon

Imagine, for a moment, if you will, living in a refugee camp, sleeping shoulder to shoulder with strangers, unable to decide which is worse, the pain, the noise, the overwhelming smell of decay and sewage, the hunger, the fear, the sense of abandonment.

~~~

Imagine, for a moment, if you will, living in a war-torn third world country, drinking untreated water, the twelve-year-old girls waiting to be raped, so they can die in childbirth before the age of thirteen, while their brothers are trained to murder.

~~~

Imagine, for a moment, if you will, living in the comfort of the West, eating breakfast and setting off for your day.

~~~

Why, one might ask, would you imagine any of it, unless you thought you could make a difference?

'Everything you can imagine is real.'

Pablo Picasso

'Imagine all the people
Living life in peace.'

John Lennon
~~~

July 25

Gratitude

'I remember, I remember,
The house where I was born,
The little window where the sun
Came peeping in at morn.'

Thomas Hood

Memories, memories. The good and the bad. Yes, there were mistakes, things that could have gone better – or for that matter worse.

We did what we did. We did what we could. And now we have uncertain memories. Happy and sad.

Regardless of what happened, we have a lot to be grateful for.

And we have this moment, Now. We have sight, hearing, feeling, a dwelling place and some food, and we can keep adding to the list.

Let the feeling of gratitude grow and shine throughout our day. Whatever we are going through, it could be worse. Moaning about it drags us down. So let's enjoy our lives as fully as we can.

'You may break, you may shatter the vase, if you will,
But the scent of the roses will hang round it still.'

Thomas Moore

' "There", he said, "You'll remember this day, my girl. For the rest of your life." "I already have." said Mary.'

Alan Garner

July 26

Living

'May I ask you what you were hoping to see out of a Torquay bedroom window? Sydney Opera House, perhaps? The Hanging Gardens of Babylon? Herds of wildebeest sweeping majestically....'

John Cleese and Connie Booth

'To travel hopefully is a better thing than to arrive, and true success is to labour.'

Robert Louis Stevenson

'Are we there yet?!' 'Are we there yet?!' Cries from the back of the car. As we grow older, we may stop asking the question aloud, but most of us don't relish the journey.

We move through our lives, waiting for the next 'good' thing to happen. And more often than not, we are disappointed when we reach it.

Sometimes we have fleeting moments of bliss, as we travel towards our death.

It's all a journey, and it is ours, it is the only one we are going to get. Why are we so impatient for it to end? Why would anyone choose to focus on the dull and dreary passage of time, rather than delighting in every superb, glorious, second of life.

'Commuter – one who spends his life
In riding to and from his wife;
A man who shaves and takes a train,
And then rides back to shave again.'

E B White

'I have not told even half of the things I have seen.'

Marco Polo

July 27

Laughter

Medvedenko: Why do you wear black all the time?
Masha: I'm in mourning for my life, I'm unhappy.

Anton Chekhov

'The most wasted of all days is that on which one has not laughed.'

Nicolas Chamfort

When we are not laughing, and others are, their laughter can be like a dentist drill, or fingernails scratching a chalkboard. And if it crosses our mind that their laughter is about us, it freezes our soul, we withdraw into blackness or lash out in anger.

Quite often, the root cause of our troubles is that we are taking ourselves – and our problems – too seriously. If someone approached us, with our troubles and our seriousness, we would want to chivvy them out of it and help them to move on from it, by laughing with them and enabling them to lighten up.

Laughing at things, even when we do not find them funny – or maybe especially when we don't think they're funny, changes them and changes us. However bleak our outlook is, others are worse off than us. Laughter is fantastic food, it creates endorphins in us, and makes the unbearable bearable.

So, if we find the laughter of others jarring, let's treat that as an early warning sign, reminding us to move to the lighter side of the road.

'You don't stop laughing because you grow old. You grow old because you stop laughing.'

Michael Pritchard

July 28

Fear

'And I will show you something different from either
Your shadow at morning striding behind you
Or your shadow at evening rising to meet you;
I will show you fear in a handful of dust.'

T S Eliot

Fear can consume and destroy us, and all about us. It can pervade everything in our lives, and slowly ruin all the things in which we once rejoiced.

Fear is like turning out the lights at dusk, our whole world becomes even greyer and clings to us like a shroud.

Any fear, however small, starts that process, and unless eliminated, spreads its shadow.

Fear is of the future. We imagine events, like a movie in our head, seeing the worst outcome, over and over and over again.

To melt, dissolve, eradicate fear, travel in your mind, beyond the event you]fear, and see the end, with a good outcome for all concerned.

It has passed. The fear and anxiety are not there.

Now come back to the present, and the fear and anxiety will no longer be there.

What happened in "the event" is not the issue, you only know that it has passed. The outcome is not the issue.

You can now relax and take whatever steps you can, to prepare for the event.

'Let me assert my firm belief that the only thing we have to fear is fear itself.'

Franklin D Roosevelt

July 29

Action

'If you want knowledge, you must take part in the practice of changing reality. If you want to know the taste of a pear, you must change the pear by eating it yourself.'

Mao Tse-tung

What if..? What if..? What if..?
If's, buts and maybes?
Such a good way to prevent any action, and fill ourselves with fear. Or to go forward at a disadvantage. Or to hand control of events over to others.
If we stop. If we take a deep breath, which we can always do. If we can go beyond the event that is "troubling", "what if-ing" us, and see ourselves ok. If we do that, then we will be able to proceed with elegance.
Enjoy.

'One of the greatest journeys in life is overcoming insecurity and learning to truly not give a shit.'

J A Konrath

July 30

Awareness

'A truth is always a compound of two half-truths and you never reach it, because there is always something more to say.'

Tom Stoppard

The truth as we know it locks us into the world as we perceive it.

However, that is, in fact, only one dimension of the world.

If we were to go for a walk with an architect, a birdwatcher, a policeman, a criminal and they explained the surroundings, as they saw them, our experience of the world would change forever.

Similarly, if we were to go out with a teenager, an octogenarian, or a child, and we took a moment to explore their perceptions, we would gain new insights.

It may not be easy, but it is rewarding. Let's go and explore the worlds of others and bring some of their delights back into our reality.

' "But the Emperor has nothing on at all!" said the little child.'

Hans Christian Andersen

July 31

Time

'Tomorrow, and tomorrow, and tomorrow,
Creeps in this petty pace from day to day.
To the last syllable of recorded time;
And all our yesterdays have lighted fools
The way to dusty death.'

William Shakespeare - Macbeth

Suppose you go into your garden. Some members of your family – your children perhaps, or parents – have a bonfire going.

How lovely. As you approach, you realise that they are throwing handfuls of banks notes onto it. £50 notes, £20 notes, in they go, burning, floating away.

You go into your garden, (perhaps more cautiously this time) and people are hacking at, destroying plants that you have lovingly nurtured and grown from seeds.

And yet isn't that what most of us do, with the most valuable, irreplaceable element in our lives – time. We can NEVER get it back. It is priceless, and we waste so much of it. Dribble it away.

Only by stopping for long enough, and deciding what to do, and by committing fully to that by then doing it, can we alter how we spend our time.

'Emily, I have a little confession to make. I really am a horse doctor. But marry me, and I'll never look at any other horse.'

Groucho Marx

Read...

Enjoy...

Share

August 1

Respect

'Any God I ever felt in church I brought in with me. And I think all the other folks did too. They come to church to share God not find God.'

Alice Walker

We share God. We share the world. We do not own either.

If we can realise that we are, at best, the handmaidens of the world, we will see that the world is not our possession. In the same way that, if a friend invites us into his house, the things there are his, we use them, respect them while we're there, and then we move on.

If we rape and pillage the world, recklessly and unnecessarily cluttering our little corner with expensive detritus, we are not respecting or caring for it.

Sadly, most of us do this, without even considering it.

Let's look after our corner. After all, if you think about it, even the air that we breathe is only on loan to us.

'What would the world be, once bereft
Of wet and wildness? Let them be left,
O let them be left, wilderness and wet;
Long live the weeds and the wildness yet.'

Gerard Manley Hopkins

'Man must choose whether to be rich in things or in the freedom to use them.'

Ivan Illich

August 2

Fear Love

'There is nothing quite as simple as recognising that every expression, every word and every action any one of us makes is motivated by one of two feelings: love or fear.'

Karen Casey

Everything is fear or love. Sounds simple, doesn't it. Let's look at it for a moment. If it's true, then everything, anger, self-pity, failure, looking down on others, lack of self-forgiveness, lying, sloth, are all fear. Does knowing this make a difference? I didn't think so.

But having examined my shortcomings, negative self-beliefs, (all fear) I realised how very liberating this is.

If they are fear and the opposite of fear is love, then to get rid of fear, all I need to do is to replace the fear with love. So when I have negative feelings I think, that's fear, and I move my mind, I change my thinking to thoughts of love. I go into the love and feel it, and the fear disappears.

If you're a visual person, replace the dark, the blackness with light, Brilliant White Light. Look at the negative and bathe it with love or light and suddenly the negative dissolves and you're left with light and love and the troubles, the darkness is no longer there.

It takes practice. The negative will reappear, but it can be bathed with light again... and again. It feels good.

And I choose to feel good, so I keep doing it until it has changed, I have changed, and the negative no longer bothers me.

'Love is letting go of fear.'

Karen Casey

'There is no illusion greater than fear.'

Lao Tzu

August 3

Criticism

'Honest criticism is hard to take – particularly when it comes from a relative, a friend, an acquaintance or a stranger.'

Franklin P. Jones

It's easy to find fault – in others. Let's face it. They just don't do things in quite the right way. And so we go to 'help' them perform 'up to our standards'.

And they still get it wrong! What a dilemma! Obviously, they must need my 'help'.

The words you find in the dictionary describing criticism include: - condemned, slagged off, denigrated, badgered, moaned at, grumbled at, nagged, hounded, trashed. If we don't want to experience any of these, why then would anyone else?

We are entitled to our opinions, and we can express them once. We can show people how to do things differently. But when we repeatedly criticise, we are just re-enforcing their behaviour.

Each time we explode about how untidy their room is, or how they sniff all the time, their unconscious hears us state it, and says to itself, 'Oh I can do that, I'm good at that' and continues to do it.

So if, for example, we want a tidy room, we start by telling everybody how tidy the room is.

If nagging worked, it would have worked already. We want to talk about what we want, not about what we don't want. If we act as if we are already getting what we want, we are far more likely to get it.

'Before you criticise someone, walk a mile in his shoes. That way, if he gets angry, he'll be a mile away – and barefoot.'

Sarah Jackson

August 4

Inventory

'I am always within myself, and it is I who am my tormentor.'

Leo Tolstoy

It is so easy to beat ourselves up, to put ourselves down. Often we do not need anybody else to point out our mistakes. We know just how to crucify ourselves.

Whether we do that or not, it is a good idea to review our day as it comes to an end to see how it went.

The traditional question is something like 'How did I f -ck up my day?', which isn't a good launching pad.

It is better to start by asking oneself 'What went well?'. And so focus on our successes however minor.

We want to congratulate ourselves for them. Congratulate with feeling.

Our unconscious loves praise and will do whatever it can to get more. So praising ourselves increases the likelihood that we will do more 'good', 'happy-making' things tomorrow.

Next, we can ask ourselves 'What could have gone better?' Which gives us the chance of thinking of improvements or amends we can make, without beating ourselves up.

Doing this ensures that we don't go to bed carrying unnecessary mental baggage and sets us up for an excellent start to our next day.

'I've always thought that you are what you are, and you shouldn't pretend to be anyone else. But Oliver used to correct me and explain that you are whoever it is you're pretending to be.'

Julian Barnes

August 5

Language

'I gotta use words when I talk to you.'

T S Eliot

'Words are, of course, the most powerful drug used by mankind.'

Rudyard Kipling

We use and hear words without always knowing their meaning.

Life is much fuller and develops new dimensions if we ask/delve/discover the meaning of new words.

Looking them up in a dictionary, or even more quickly on our phone, is not only fun but rewarding.

Some people challenge themselves to learn a new word every day.

With the vast number of swear words that are used these days as adjectives and nouns, it is fun to become more erudite.

'One forgets words as one forgets names. One's vocabulary needs constant fertilizing, or it will die.'

Evelyn Waugh

'Some word that teems with hidden meaning – like 'Basingstoke'.'

W S Gilbert

August 6

Growth

'I can't do with any more education. I was full up years ago.'

P G Wodehouse

'What I know is enough for me.'

Perseus 34-64 AD

So many people know it – all. And have stopped thinking. So much more comfortable to think about the new car, a new kitchen, celebs, football, soaps, or even just how busy and exhausted they are. So sad.

When we could be exploring the world, new ideas, and challenging ourselves to find out more.

Watching a documentary is far better than lying back and letting a soap wash over us. Most TV is just chewing gum for the mind.

But learning, knowledge, understanding needs more than just a little splash of information. It requires action and interaction from us – the desire to explore what's out there and to drink it up.

That is what keeps us alive and growing. We are either growing or decaying. And when we think we know it all, or can't be bothered we're dying.

'Education is not the filling of a pale, but the lighting of a fire.'

W B Yeats

'We used to think that if we knew one, we knew two, because one and one are two. We are finding out that we must learn a great deal more about 'and'.'

Arthur Eddington

August 7

Assertiveness

'There were times when it seemed to him that the different parts of him were not all under the same management.'

Russell Hoban

Others have their perception of us, and if we go along with them, we are purely being the type of person they are creating. If our parents, boss, spouse make us cringe and obey them, we are losing our right to be independent. If they or our friends (?) treat us as a buffoon, a dolly bird, a womaniser, a housewife, a macho man, we buy into their stereotype, and believe them.

These become our beliefs about ourselves. A vast number of the ideas we have about ourselves, we have probably inherited from our parents, grand-parents, or even further back - our beliefs about how we should behave and what we can do or become.

The longer we continue to believe these things, without question, the harder it is to rise above and change them. (The stereotypes that I listed above may not apply to you, however, but are you free of the more subtle labels that are foisted upon you and adopted without thought?)

We have probably forgotten who we are, but we know we are not as we present ourselves. If we want to change, we can. We will fight it. We don't like having our beliefs changed. And as we change, our relationship with other people in our lives will change too. And they unwittingly will do their best to keep us stuck.

It is worth it. It is marvelous to become the person that we can be, to cease being a shadow, just obeying the lies that we have lived. Have courage. Explore. Become.

'Why not go out on a limb? That's where the fruit is.

Mark Twain

August 8

Truth

'Beware lest you lose the substance by grasping at the shadow.'

Aesop

'We talked a lot about life. There was nothing else to talk about.'

Amanda Vail

We (sometimes) talk about life, truth, the meaning of life. We may even wonder about it from time to time. (And if we don't, then it can't be a problem.)

The beautiful thing about all those questions is that there are probably no answers – no definitive answers.

It's likely that if there is 'truth' it's within us, it's been there all the time, we are just blind to it, or maybe blinded by it.

Probably the only way we can put a mental finger on it is by going inside into the inner knowledge within us and the peace that exists there.

While we may find it, we cannot understand it with words.

The real truth is wordless. Simply accept the inexplicable / the unknown. It is worth the hunt, the surrender, and peace that it brings when we bathe in it.

'Errors like straws, upon the surface flow:
He who would search for pearls must dive below.'

John Dryden

August 9th

Create

Silence

August 10

Rules

'He shunts aside all rules, regulations and dicta, except for the three laws he says a nice old Negro Lady once taught him: Never play cards with anyone called 'Doc'. Never eat at any place called 'Moms'. And never, ever, no matter what else you do in your whole life, never sleep with anyone whose troubles are worse than your own.'

Nelson Algren

'What do you do sir?' asked a boy from the back of the class. 'if your girlfriend's troubles get worse than yours after you've been with her for a while?'

And so undoubtedly, it's best to have no rules. And yet we do. Many of them very helpful, no doubt. But only if we can be open about them and are able to question them.

We know how the dishwasher should be loaded, but if a guest does it differently, what then?

We know how to drive from A to B, but what if a cab driver takes a different route?

We know the order a meal should be eaten in but what if someone eats their pudding first?

Do we ever question the things we know? Do we allow ourselves freedom of thought?

'Life is not a problem to be solved, but a mystery to be lived.'

Thomas Merton

August 11

Responsible

'Each man the architect of his own fate.'

Appius Claudius Caecus

If we don't like our current situation or there are aspects of it that we don't like, we can choose to change them. If we don't decide to change them, then we would be well advised to realise that we have chosen them and so accept them.

Sometimes we are in a situation that we don't choose to be in, and that we cannot change. We can, however, decide how we exist within it. We can dwell on the negatives, the unfairness, all the bad aspects, and in so doing make it worse. And time crawls by, and it drags us down.

Or we can focus on the good things, the blessings, however small they are. If we get food, that is a blessing, however bad it is. If we can see daylight, that is a blessing, even if there is only a small crack that it shines through. And choosing to focus on the benefits strengthens us, gives us courage and time passes more quickly.

'For man is man and master of his fate.'

Alfred, Lord Tennyson

August 12

Meditation

'We have a beautiful
mother
Her green lap
immense
Her brown embrace
eternal
Her blue body
everything
we know.'

Alice Walker

Here's a simple two-minute meditation. Or for as long as you want.

Sit. Count from 3 to 1. Relax, be at peace.

Let the earth - Mother Earth - act as a magnet. Let it draw all the blackness, negativity, out of you, through the soles of your feet.

Let that the Brilliant White Light, which is Universal Unconditional Love and Healing, flow into you. Let it replace the blackness, so that you become a brilliant white radiant being, with the light filling you and shining out of you, radiating into the world.

Prepare yourself for whatever is coming up in your day.

And come back into the world and get on with your life - spreading light wherever you go.

'Everything is shown up by being exposed to the light, and whatever is exposed to the light, itself becomes light.'

St Paul

August 13

Hell

'Me miserable! which way shall I fly
Infinite wrath, and infinite despair?
Which way I fly is hell; myself am hell;
And in th' lowest deep a lower deep
Still threatening to devour me opens wide,
To which the hell I suffer seems a heav'n.'

John Milton

Oh where is hell? Where do we need to go to live there? Why would we ever choose to concede victory to despair?

I have a friend whose daughter, after travelling around Europe with her boyfriend, entered into a suicide pact with him. They both died. And yet love and money were waiting for her at home had she asked.

So who's in hell now? Certainly, my friend who loved and loved and loved her daughter is now in hell. Maybe her love was her crime. Perhaps her love suffocated her daughter. Life on earth can be hell, and it must have been for them. Death must have promised some relief.

We have to give people freedom, however much we love and want to protect them. When a friend commits suicide, we feel sorrow and anger. Why didn't he call? I would have helped. Wherever we are on our journey through our life, however horrendous it may appear to us, there are always others that we can help and love. Only we can give freedom to ourselves.

'The doors of heaven and hell are adjacent and identical: both green, both beautiful.'

Nikos Kazantzakis

'Heaven and Hell are Just One Breath Away.'

Andy Warhol

August 14

Thoughts

'Counting the beats,
Counting the slow heart beats,
The bleeding to death of time in slow heart beats,
Wakeful they lie.'

Robert Graves

The sleepless nights. Or waking in the middle, tortured by thoughts, that churn and spin like giant dead spiders blown round and round a drum. You catch one, look at it, discard it then grab another, and another until the first one returns to laugh at you again.

Thoughts that are not anchored, fly by, time and time again. They needn't be horrors, perhaps just the mundane. Buy potatoes, talk to Fred, pay the gas bill, wash the green... buy potatoes.... gas bill.... potatoes.... They crowd out sleep until you do finally drift off, half an hour before you are due to drag yourself out of bed.

You don't need to do this. You simply need a list. Put everything on the list. The thoughts are then anchored. If you think of something that isn't on the list, turn on the light and add it. Say to yourself, 'I don't need to think about that, it's on the list'. If you think of something that is on the list, e.g. buy potatoes, say, 'there is nothing I can do about that now, it's on the list! What I need to do now is go to sleep, so that I can awake tomorrow feeling rested and able to deal with the things I need to do.' And then go to sleep.

If necessary, repeat to yourself, that you cannot do anything about it now. Go to sleep. Say 'Sleep' to yourself on each out-breath, as you relax into the bedding.

'Don't try to solve serious matters in the middle of the night.

Philip K Dick

August 15

Awareness

'We are no more responsible for evil thoughts which pass through our minds, than a scarecrow for the birds which fly over the seed-plot he has to guard; the sole responsibility in each case is to prevent them from settling.'

John Churton Collins

If we want to grow spiritually, then we want to guard our thoughts and actions vigilantly. It is important not to let 'Wrong Thoughts' settle, but to let them fly right on by. And the more we do this, the fewer will pass.

To be conscious of our thoughts and shortcomings can be more difficult. Often, our faults have become habits that we simply don't notice, the slight put-downs, wisps of irritation, our self- importance. (Or maybe our faults are vast, like a hurricane roaring through the world, destroying everything that's in its path. I don't know, but you might.)

If we are to grow spiritually, not only do we want to guard against our thoughts, but we want to discuss our life with someone.

The man who counsels himself has a fool for a counsellor. We need to discuss ourselves with someone else. We cannot honestly see ourselves.

'Isn't it strange that we talk least about the things we think about most.'

Charles A Lindberg

August 16

Failure

'She knows there's no success like failure
And that failure's no success at all.'

Bob Dylan

All the mobile phone cameras are at the ready. The relations collected, five grandparents, one great grandparent. Baby Jake is going to walk, to take his first step.

A hush descends, Jake pushes his left foot forward, wobbles, holds on, he lets go, lifts one foot. He falls!

Daddy rushes forward and picks up little Jake by his pants and throws him into his cot. "Right there you are!" he cries "You've had your chance, you've failed. That's it!"

Everybody goes home, and Jake never leaves his cot.

Is that how it happened for you?

No?

And yet we beat ourselves up so horribly when we fail.

Let's forgive ourselves, jump up, dust ourselves off and move on.

Only the people who do nothing, never fail.

'Half the failures in life arise from pulling in one's horse as he is leaping.'

Julian & Augustus Hare

'This is the first of punishments, that no guilty man is acquitted if judged by himself.'

Juvenal

August 17

Habits

'We are what we repeatedly do. Excellence, then, is not an act, but a habit.'

Aristotle

It stands to reason then that the opposite of 'Excellence' is also a habit.

Practice makes permanent. It doesn't necessarily, in fact, it rarely ever, makes perfect.

But we trundle thoughtlessly through our lives, strengthening our habits, and believing that we are doing the best that can.

If we have a habit, we want to get rid of, we cannot just give it up. Nature abhors a vacuum, and it will not let one exist, so the only way to change a habit is to replace it, with a new one.

Perhaps if we look at the things we always do – we might on a clear day, be able to spot some room for improvement. We might even, with help and discussion if necessary, be able to identify something else to do instead. Then, like an explorer, we can feel the excitement of moving one foot forward on our journey. And begin.

When we catch ourselves 'doing' the old habit, we say "I don't do that anymore, I used to.... (whatever the old habit was), but now I.... (whatever the new habit is). Each time we do the new habit, it strengthens, it becomes closer to being our new reality.

'Habit with him was all the test of truth
"It must be right: I've done it from my youth"'

George Crabbe

August 18

Self-Acceptance

'I am not at all the sort of person you and I took me for.'

Jane Carlyle

'Am I as good as them?'

'Do I do that as well as they do?'

These questions flit across our minds.

In terms of some things, games, for example, it's obvious. And if we want to improve in those areas, we want to do them with people who are better than us.

Most things are unjudgeable. Are they better parents, children, or friends, for example? Who is creating the yardstick?

Is it something that we can realistically live up to? We want to discover that we can never do 'our best' and accept what we do. We want to stop telling others to do their best. Encourage them to, just do, and to enjoy the doing.

Another set of questions we might ask are, is my meditation, peace of mind, closeness to God, harmony with the world, as good as 'his'?

If 'he' is very good at them, 'he' may be able to help us to improve.

But the bottom line is, are we searching within, to be at one with ourselves, fully? Nothing else matters.

'Talent develops in quiet places, character in the full current of human life.'

Johann Wolfgang von Goethe

'A propensity to hope and joy is real riches: One to fear and sorrow real poverty.'

David Hume

August 19

Experience

'The troubles of the young are soon over; they leave no external mark. If you wound the tree in its youth the bark will quickly cover the gash; but when the tree is very old, peeling the bark off, and looking carefully, you will see the scar is there still.'

Olive Schreiner

Oh the scars of life, still waiting to trip us up unexpectedly, like a rock on a path at dusk. Most of the time we can walk by without even noticing them, and then suddenly – There! – Enveloping us!

Like all troubles, they can either drag us down or build us up. Weaken or strengthen us. Indeed without them, we would be less, we would know and understand less.

If we can learn to use them for strength, they add to the armoury we have to help others, and in turn ourselves.

'One writes of scars healed, a loose parallel to the pathology of the skin, but there is no such thing in the life of an individual. There are open wounds, shrunk sometimes to the size of a pinprick but wounds still. The marks of suffering are more comparable to the loss of a finger or the sight of an eye. We may not miss them, either, for one minute in the year, but if we should, there is nothing to be done about it.'

F Scott Fitzgerald

August 20

Emotions

'Undisciplined squads of emotion.'

T S Eliot

'One may not regard the world as a sort of metaphysical brothel for emotions.'

Arthur Koestler

What beautiful things – love, kindness, honesty, trust, patience, generosity.

And yet so easily abused. We give them, but we add strings. We expect things back in return. We smother our family, friends with our love so that they cannot breathe or live freely.

The other side of the coin is taking advantage of them, gobbling up their generosity, love, kindness, and trust, using it to our advantage, without returning it.

Maybe we are guilty of neither, perhaps one or two, but only a 'little'. Only we know. (Actually, others may know too, but that is not the issue here). If we are transgressing, we want to ask ourselves why.

'Now that my ladder's gone
I must lie down where all the ladders start
In the foul rag-and-bone shop of the heart.'

W B Yeats

August 21

Freedom

'You took my freedom from me long ago, and you can't give it back because you have no freedom yourself.'

Alexander Solzhenitsyn

'If you love somebody set them free.'

Sting

So few are free. We are controlled by others, and we, in turn, control others too. We make demands. If we limit another's freedom we are no longer free ourselves. The ropes that bind them, bind us too.

At home, at work, in our day to day lives, we create rules that prevent our freedom and enslave our fellow travellers.

If we can find it within ourselves to release them, we too can be free. Free to grow, to become, to be, to live.

If we are controlled by others, we can still choose to be free. We may not be able to decide the things we will have to do, but we can always choose how we feel about them. We can find the positive in any situation.

Freedom has dignity. Without freedom, we are likely to be pulled beneath the waves by negativity.

'Since freedom is no more than a sensation, what difference is there between being free and believing ourselves free?'

E M Cioran

'The moment the slave resolves that he will no longer be a slave, his fetters fall. He frees himself and shows the way to others. Freedom and slavery are mental states.'

Mahatma Gandhi

August 22

Meditation

'I throw myself down in my chamber, and I call in and invite God, and his Angels thither, and when they are there, I neglect God and his Angels, for the noise of a fly, for the rattling of a coach, for the whining of a door.'

John Donne

We're human, frail beings, full of good intentions and failures.

To achieve any spirituality is difficult. There are three cornerstones, a personal inventory, for if we don't attempt to look at ourselves, to see how we are getting on, how can we expect to advance. We want to celebrate our successes as well as looking at our shortcomings, and we want to identify places where we can improve.

The other two cornerstones are prayer and meditation. Talking and listening, with thought.

They do not need to take hours, they just need to be long enough. We need all three, otherwise, it's like taking a bath without washing, or washing but failing to rinse.

'Oh, I just keep plugging away. At best it's like being in a dark room with someone you love. You can't see them; but you know they're there.'

Cardinal Basil Hulme

August 23

Love

'Breathless, we flung us on the windy hill,
Laughed in the sun, and kissed the lovely grass.'

Rupert Brooke

Obviously, lovers, filled with that total joy of the moment.

However strongly it burns, it's fleeting, leaving us with memories and emotions.

On special days (when the atmospheric conditions are right) the jets leave lines and crosses in the sky.

Shortly after my Mother died, I was walking across a field, and I saw crosses in the sky. They are kisses from my Mother, I thought, so ever since then, when I see crosses in the sky, that's how I think of them.

So please accept this gift from me to you, from now on, whenever you see crosses in the sky, let them be kisses to you from someone precious.

Here is another gift if you would like it. The next time you have an apple, cut it in half, not through the stalk, but across it. Inside you will find a star, let the star be a gift for you, from someone you love. So each time you eat an apple....

Whether you want these gifts for yourself or not, give them away to people you love, so that they may have your kisses and stars.

Let's create a world of people receiving kisses and stars and love.

'They gave it to me.... For an un-birthday present.'

Lewis Carroll

August 24

Perception

'Impossible is a word only to be found in the dictionary of fools.'

Napoleon Bonaparte

When we were young, there were times when anything seemed possible, and times where the simplest things seemed impossible.

We learned that there were limits and what sometimes seemed impossible, was often easy.

And so we reach today, and the trouble with today is that we think we know our limitations. We know what we can and cannot do. And we choose what we will, or we will not do.

If we were to re-assess, to allow the idea of possibilities in, we might find that our lives could be so much fuller, richer, and more abundant.

And lack of time is not an excuse, because if you want to get something done, you ask someone busy to do it, not the person who has all the time in the world.

'We think too small. Like the frog at the bottom of the well. He thinks the sky only as big as the top of the well. If he surfaced, he would have an entirely different view.'

Mao Tse-tung

August 25

Being

'As a flower springs up secretly in a fenced garden, known to no cattle, bruised by no plough, caressed by the winds, strengthened by the sun, and drawn up by the shower, so many a boy and many a girl desire it.'

Catullus

As soon as we give something a name, a label, we change it. We see it as one of many, rather than as an individual miracle.

Here's a challenge.

Go and look at a flower today. Discard its label and all expectations about it, just go and spend time discovering it. Look deeply into it, become one with it. Discover things about that flower that you have never experienced before.

'How long should I do it for?'

Do it until you wonder if you have been doing it long enough, and then do it for at least as long again.

Lose yourself in it. Go so deeply into it, that you completely forget about yourself, and you are only thinking about the flower.

That period of ceasing to be you is magnificent. It is oneness with the world. It is a gateway to being.

Delight in it.

Go there often.

'I haven't got a flower'

Use something else.

'Thou unassuming common place
Of nature'

William Wordsworth

August 26

Letting Go

'I never gave away anything without wishing I had kept it; nor kept anything without wishing I had given it away.

Louise Brooks

It is so easy to surround ourselves with clutter. To live with things we never use or wear.

'I'd better keep it just in case....'

It is painful, to take that step, to let go, to say goodbye.

And as it starts to go, we want to claw it back.... just in case....

The reward for letting go?

Freedom.

Mental, physical, and spiritual freedom, joy, a feeling of release and then relief.

There is another bonus, we now have some space for new things, but before we re-clutter, it's worth spending time enjoying the space. And realising that every time we get something, we are sacrificing that delightful emptiness.

'Everything should be made as simple as possible but no simpler.'

Albert Einstein

August 27

Arrogance

'She developed a persistent troubled frown which gave her the expression of someone who is trying to repair a watch with his gloves on.'

James Thurber

Sometimes, even the best of us, start something the wrong way. And the temptation is to carry on regardless, struggling against the odds.

So much better to stop, to reconsider and admit we might have been wrong. Much better to get advice, help and to start again.

It is so easy to fool ourselves into believing that we know best and that we know what other people need and want.

Arrogance is a significant contributor to failure.

It is so easy to spot it in others, and so very hard to conceive of it in ourselves.

Even harder, if you're not looking.

' "Alf Todd," said Ukridge, soaring to an impressive burst of imagery, "has about as much chance as a one-armed blind man in a dark room trying to shove a pound of melted butter into a wild cat's left ear with a red-hot needle." '

P G Wodehouse

August 28

Challenge

'About the only thing that comes to us without effort is old age.'

Gloria Pitzer

It is fun to challenge ourselves. To find one thing every day that we can do slightly better, or a little bit more of, so that we can see the improvement. *

Many of us do challenge ourselves endlessly and push ourselves further and further in our quest to succeed.

But most of us don't. We just do what we did yesterday, enough to get us through until tomorrow.

* (And I am not talking about eating doughnuts here!)

If we would like to move out of the ranks of 'the most', all we need to do to start is to find one simple thing to work on and to improve.

For example, if we were to increase the distance we walked every day by ten steps, or lowered the time it took us to walk somewhere by ten seconds, or put 5% less sugar in our coffee. If we then continued to do it, we would have achieved something.

Choose your own thing. Have fun with it. Enjoy the challenge. Bask in the achievement.

'The world is an oyster, but you don't crack it open on a mattress.'

Arthur Miller

'Nobody ever drowned in his own sweat.'

Ann Landers

August 29

Peace

'The wolf also shall dwell with the lamb, and the leopard shall lie down with the kid; and the calf and the young lion and the fatling together, and a little child shall lead them.'

Isaiah II:6

We all have within us, the wolf and the lamb, the lion and the calf, and at different times, one or another of them scrambles to the surface and takes control.

'Why did I do that?' We sometimes wonder.

We also encourage the calf or the lion of others to rise up in them, and confront us, or submit (albeit unwillingly).

Sometimes (if we're clever) we can still our minds and become aware of what is driving us or others, and then take the necessary steps to find peace within us. Meditation is good, or just stopping the endless nonsense that goes on inside our heads.

'The lion and the calf shall lie down together, but the calf won't get much sleep.'

Woody Allen

'No absolute is going to make the lion lie down with the lamb: unless the lamb is inside.'

D H Lawrence

August 30

Emptiness

'How does it feel
To be on your own
With no direction home
Like a complete unknown
Like a rolling stone?'

Bob Dylan

Most of us have moments of being lost, if not today, then last year or next month. Times when things don't feel quite right, when we know that we want something, but we don't know what.

The truth is that new objects, new direction, might distract us from the feeling, without actually filling the hole.

We are more than just physical beings, we are spiritual beings too, and the cause of our inner disquiet is probably not physical, it is undoubtedly spiritual. The trouble is, we do all we can to fill the gap, and hide the spiritual side of our being.

When we feel disquiet, rather than looking for external solutions, use meditation to change the way you feel.

'Few people can say: I am here. They look for themselves in the past and see themselves in the future.'

Georges Braque

August 31

Achievement

'The worst is not,
So long as one can say, "This is the worst" '

William Shakespeare – King Lear

'The beginning of hardship is like the first taste of bitter food – it seems for a moment unbearable: yet, if there is nothing else to satisfy our hunger, we take another bite and find it possible to go on.'

George Eliot

Long-distance runners talk about hitting a wall at some stage in their run when every part of their mind and body wants to shut down and quit. And yet, if they push themselves through the wall, it all becomes much easier.

There are walls in many areas of our lives, and in the things we undertake. We reach moments when we feel a great desire to quit.

Whenever we embark on a new project, we are likely to arrive at a time when it feels as if things are not going as well as we wanted them to, or it begins to feel boring, just too much effort (today). We find ourselves using all our ingenuity to find ways and reasons to stop.

This is normal, it is our wall, all we need to do is to drive ourselves through it, and the undertaking will become exciting and fun again.

'What does not kill me makes me stronger.'

Friedrich Nietzsche

'Scars have the strange power to remind us that our past is real.'

Cormac McCarthy

Enjoying?

Share

This

Book

With

Someone

Else

September 1

Fulfilment

'Fear has always been a diminisher of life, whether bred in the bogs of superstition or clothed in the brocades of dogma and ritual, the spectre of death has reduced the living to supplicants, powerless.'

Marya Mannes

Some people don't want us to succeed!

Yes, it's true.

Of course they won't admit that, and may not even realise that they want you to fail.

They may do it in obvious ways, but more often than not they just use their indifference or silence to control, to make you feel less, or unimportant.

The idea that they don't want you to succeed may not have even crossed your mind, but you see that if/when you do succeed it will alter the status quo of your relationship. And they cannot stand the idea of that.

If you realise that this is happening to you, you want to find someone else to be your ally, to help you to retain your focus.

Keep your dream alive, dare to walk into the sunlight – it does not matter if they will not follow.

'Probably it's true what you think, and you know.... But I don't caareeee I'm a fake character.'

Deyth Banger

'Bigotry tries to keep truth safe in its hand
With a grip that kills it.'

Rabindranath Tagore

September 2

Language

'Go to Jail. Directly to Jail. Do not pass Go. Do not collect £200.00

Monopoly

We hate being told what to do. Our parents and our teachers did it. Now we do it to ourselves.

'You've got to do this,' 'You must do that,' 'You should be doing something else', and so it goes on.

Must, got to, ought to, should, have to etc. are all authority words, and when we hear them, we dig our heels in, we rebel, and part of us thinks f**k off, leave me alone.

Experiment with me. I'm going to use 'go to work', but if that is not appropriate to you, please use some action that you are not keen on, for example, 'putting the dustbins out'.

Please say to yourself 'I've got to go to work' and see how that makes you feel inside. Then repeat the process with 'I must go to work', and 'I should go to work'. Now you have three feelings, one for each sentence.

And now say 'I want to go to work'. How does that make you feel? Different.

We want to discard all the authority words in our lives, particularly in our self-talk, and replace them with the word 'want'. It will make a tremendous difference to your well-being and your accomplishments. You also want to use the word want when making suggestions to your spouse, children, co-workers etc. You'll find they are far more willing to do what you're suggesting.

'Not in the clamor of the crowded street,
Not in the shouts and plaudits of the throng,
But in ourselves, are triumph and defeat.'

H W Longfellow

September 3

Conversation

'When you have nothing to say, say nothing.'

Charles Colton

Unfortunately, most people don't know that they have nothing to say.

And what they do say, more often than not – is a jumble of complaints and negative opinions.

What can we do, when faced with such an onslaught – Always assuming we are not also the perpetrators of the crime.

We can say – if we have the courage – "If you don't have anything positive to say, say nothing." This usually works, for a while, though it may need repeating from time to time.

We can choose to spend less time 'coffee housing' with the 'Negs'.

We can change the subject to less contentious rubbish.

And we can certainly choose not to participate and add to the conflagration.

We can learn to not listen.

'There is no sin except stupidity.'

Oscar Wilde

'You can exclude noise by sound proofing your mind.'

Harold Ross

September 4

Equality

‘ “Who’s I’m Bill?”
“A Stranger!”
“ ’Eave ’arf a brick at ’im.” ’

Punch

Fear and antagonism. Such natural behaviours. Even when we’ve overcome them, there is still an initial judgement when we meet new people.

As we move further into any relationship, there is give and take. Is it equal? Or do we feel we are put upon, or conversely, are we the one who has the most benefit from the relationship.

There are equal relationships, where this does not apply, but for most of us, either we are taking advantage of others, or they are not treating us with the respect we deserve. When this is happening, we want to take stock, re-evaluate the situation and then do what we can to bring equality into it.

We may be reluctant to do this because change requires effort and confronting ourselves and others. But as we all know, nothing ventured, nothing gained.

‘Strive not to be a success, but rather to be of value.’

Albert Einstein

‘You miss 100% of the shots you don’t take.’

Wayne Gretzky

September 5

Chance

'I seem to have been only like a boy playing on the seashore, and diverting myself in now and then finding a smoother pebble or a prettier shell than ordinary, while the great ocean of truth lay all undiscovered before me.'

Sir Isaac Newton

We cling to the things and people we have as if they were the only ones that could have been in our lives.

Our wives, husbands, friends, children are incredibly precious and important to us. We feel as if they are irreplaceable, and in many ways, they are.

But if we think back to the circumstances that started our relationships, had we turned left, instead of right, had we caught the next train, got a different job, not gone to that party, then our lives could have been completely different. We could be different, and with other people, whom we would love as little (or as much).

Yes, the people in our lives are special. But everyone was an accident. So we want to remain open to new accidents and not unnecessarily tied to the old ones.

'If you should ask me where I've been all this time, I have to say, "Things happen." '

Pablo Neruda

September 6

Guilt

'If we had no faults of our own we would not take so much pleasure in noticing those of others.'

François Duc de La Rochefoucauld

It is easy to criticise. And some people have a habit of using criticism and guilt to control us. We can chase our tails, but even if we were to catch them, we would not have succeeded in their eyes. They say something, and we instantly feel the discomfort of guilt in our body.

There is a solution. The next time they criticise you, look them in the eye and say, 'You're not trying to make me feel guilty, are you?'

They will almost certainly say 'No, no of course not', and you will have started to break through the chain of guilt.

When they do it again, repeat the question 'You're not trying to make me feel guilty, are you?' And gradually they will learn not to do it anymore.

If they admit that they do want to make you feel guilty, you want to discuss it with them, and then decide if you wish put up with it anymore. You may choose to accept the relationship but choose not to accept the feeling of guilt.

If by chance, you are using guilt to manipulate others, perhaps you should ask the question of yourself. Can you look yourself in the eye and do that? Do you want to make others miserable to achieve your own ends?

'Those who would make us feel, must feel themselves."

Charles Churchill

'Man's inhumanity to man
Makes countless thousands mourn.'

Robert Burns

September 7

Love

'This above all; to thine own self be true,
And it must follow, as the night the day,
Thou canst not then be false to any man.'

William Shakespeare – Hamlet

To be true to ourselves, we have to like, love and nurture ourselves. When we do, we can act towards others with love and compassion, understanding and support.

If we are preoccupied with ourselves, we no longer interact with other people in a worthwhile way.

We want to learn to treat others properly, to understand their frustrations, difficulties, and needs, without judging them.

When we look at others with acceptance and love, we not only enhance their lives, we enrich our own.

'You know very well that love is, above all, the gift of oneself.

Jean Anouilh

September 8

Friends

'When I was a kid, I had two friends, and they were imaginary, and they would only play with each other.'

Rita Rudner

There are many times when we are alone, and we feel alone. We may not be lonely, but we feel needy.

And we scroll through the friends, people we know in our minds/phone and think who can I contact?

It may not even be that we have anything deeply troubling us, but we feel the need for a little real honest sustenance.

We go through the list, and discard the people, until... until we have to go back to the top and start again.

It is at moments like this, if you ever experience them, when perhaps the best course of action is to stop. Stop trawling through the list, and take a few moments, maybe even a lot of moments, to go inside... oneself.

To meditate or pray, to hands one's life over to the care of a power greater than ourselves, to relax and feel free, to be at one with ourselves, to experience peace, and the pleasure of solitude.

And doing that, if we still want to contact someone, the criteria for contacting them will have changed, because our needs will have changed.

'I have lost friends, some by death... others through sheer inability to cross the street.'

Virginia Woolf

September 9

Faults

'Do not think of your faults, still less of others' faults, look for what is good and strong, and try to imitate it. Your faults will drop off, like dead leaves, when their time comes.'

John Ruskin

We strengthen what we dwell on. The past is gone. By going over it, we keep it alive and prevent our ability to move on.

If we continuously pick the scab off a wound and poke around in it, it will never heal.

Only by taking positive action can we truly move on. Others have been where we are, and they can help us. In the future, we will be able to use our strength to help others.

'Look to what is good and strong', let that be the way of life.

'The reward of a thing well done, is to have done it.'

Ralph Waldo Emmerson

'None climbs so high as he who knows not whither he is going.

Oliver Cromwell

September 10

Expectations

'Modern man lives under the illusion that he knows what he wants, while he actually wants what he is supposed to want.'

Erich Fromm

By and large, we get what we expect, but we don't necessarily get what we want.

If we think about it, run a few movies of our lives through our minds... we will see that we went there, did that, etc. and usually we experienced what we expected to experience.

Whereas we think of the things we want, along the lines of, 'It would be nice if...' but it doesn't happen because we don't expect it.

To make things happen, aside from changing the things we do, we want to change our expectations.

To take a mundane example, we're on our way to meet someone, and we don't really want to go, we expect to be bored, so sure enough we are. If we change our expectation, believe that we might have fun, then we are likely to approach the evening quite differently.

So we want to remember to choose the expectations that we want, not the ones we don't want.

'You have wants the way other people have toothache. Kind of dull and general.'

Christopher Hampton

'I'll tell you what I want, what I really really want.'

Spice Girls

September 11

Worry

'Nothing puzzles me more than time or space; and yet nothing troubles me less, as I never think about them.'

Charles Lamb

Things that trouble us need to be looked at, not ignored.

If we are concerned and do nothing, the worry will only increase. So instead of stuffing it in the back of a cupboard, we want to take action to identify, and understand, what it is that is troubling us. Only then can we do anything about it.

Sometimes we need advice.

Some worries are about others, and we want to find the best way we can offer emotional support and love.

But whatever needs doing, we want to clear it away, so that we can move on. Undealt with concerns fester and grow with inactivity.

'If one does not know to which port one is sailing, no wind is favourable.'

Seneca (The Younger)

September 12

Self-image

' "If you don't go to other men's funerals," he told Father stiffly, "they won't go to yours." '

Clarence Day

You go into a church, to a funeral. The coffin is open, and you walk up to it, to see who's funeral it is.

You are in the coffin.

The first person, from a queue of people, goes to the front and starts to speak about you.

What do they say?

Do they say what you would like them to be saying?

If not, take a little time and write down what you do want them to be saying.

What do you need to change about yourself, so that when the time comes, they will say the things you would like them to say?

What are you going to do about it?

Just reading this and thinking 'Oh yes' will not change anything.

'Not a drum was heard, not a funeral note,
As his course to the rampart we hurried.'

Charles Wolfe

'And closing the door with the delicate caution of one brushing flies off a sleeping Venus, he passed out of my life.'

P G Wodehouse

September 13

Reality

'Take care, your worship, those things over there are not giants but windmills.'

Miguel de Cervantes

The way we view things today and the way we expect things to be tomorrow creates our reality and has a profound effect on our lives.

Do you know what your reality is? Do you understand that the way you view things is not the way everyone else does?

Have you ever considered the fact that you can change your world, by changing the way you view things and by changing your behaviour?

So often, we go through life blinkered, seeing only a tiny portion of the world. We are led by our noses, from one moment to the next.

The scope of the world is truly vast. We can choose to bathe in it or continue to exist in a muddy puddle.

Even if there are restrictions in our lives that we cannot, today, escape from, we can change what we read, watch, and the content of our thoughts and conversations.

We can step into the world and delight in the sunlight, or hide in the darkness that is not reality.

'The white horse you see in the park could be a zebra synchronized with the railings.'

Ann Jellicoe

September 14

Agreement

'Diplomacy is the art of saying "Nice Doggie!" till you can find a rock.'

Will Rogers

Sometimes we find ourselves agreeing to things that we don't want to do. Similarly, we sometimes manoeuvre others into doing the things we want. And both are probably okay if they're infrequent.

However, both sow the potential seed of resentment, which can easily flourish into a mighty tree.

We want to learn to be able to say 'No' to people when it is appropriate, and maybe, even more importantly, we want to beware of forcing others into doing things they don't want to do.

There are times when we're right, and they're wrong, and they enjoy doing what we've suggested. But there are also situations where this isn't the case. We want to be on our guard against antagonizing the ones we care about.

'One of the things I learned when I was negotiating was that until I changed myself, I could not change others.'

Nelson Mandela

'You only find complete unanimity in a cemetery.'

Abel Aganbegyan

September 15

H A L T

'Time for a little something.'

A A Milne

'Anger is a brief madness.'

Horace

When we get Hungry, Angry, Lonely, or Tired, we cease to operate at our best. And if we don't do anything to change, it gets worse, along with our behaviour and feelings.

It's not difficult to make changes to bring ourselves back to equilibrium.

The only challenge is recognising the cause and stopping or HALTing before it becomes a serious problem.

'A small man can be just as exhausted as a great man.'

Arthur Miller

'Men's legs have a terribly lonely life – standing in the dark in your trousers all day.'

Ken Dodd

September 16

Meditation

'What lies behind us and what lies before us are tiny matters compared to what lies within us.'

Henry Stanley Haskins

How do we find what lies within? How do we let it out? How can we achieve peace, even if it is only fleeting?

Stop. No stop. No really stop. Stop everything.

Take a deep breath and go within.

Feel your inner energy and feel your breath flowing in and out.

Stop listening to your thoughts, just concentrate on your inner energy and your breathing.

Let that Brilliant White Light that is Universal Unconditional Love and Healing flow into you fill you, and radiate out of you.

Continue for as long as you wish.

Repeat during the day.

Continue, at some level, to do this when you come back to your day. Take your focus away from yourself and onto other people.

Ask yourself not, what can I get out of them, but instead what can I do for them? How can I improve their experience of life?

None of this is hard to achieve. It is just hard to remember to do it.

'Wherever your heart is, that is where you'll find your treasure.'

Paul Coelho

September 17

Decisions

'I shall be telling this with a sigh
Somewhere ages and ages hence:
Two roads diverged in a wood, and I –
I took the one less travelled by,
And that has made all the difference.'

Robert Frost

A man had a recurring dream:-

He was walking down a poorly lit road at night, and as he passed an alleyway on his right, he looked down it and saw two men with truncheons or metal bars attacking an unarmed man. He found himself starting to run down the alleyway to save the man, while his mind was shouting at him 'Don't go! Don't go!'

And he woke up.

We have choices, and often we do not want to make them. We chose to do nothing rather than to do the things we know we should.

Sometime later the man (who is not particularly big, muscular, or brave) found himself walking down a poorly lit street, and on his right, there was an alleyway. And down the alley, in the shadows, there were two men about to attack someone...

Decisions. What one do we take? Can we bear to live with ourselves if we take the wrong one?

'Decisions are easier you know when there are no choices left.'

P V Narasimha Rao

September 18

Deceit

' "What is truth?" said jesting Pilate, and would not stay for an answer.'

Francis Bacon

Sometimes we find it hard to admit we are wrong.

Of course, it's a habit that has long roots, wrapped in fear.

Mother 'Did you break that?' Child 'No'

It is a knee jerk reaction to being caught out. 'Someone hit the car while it was in the car park.' 'They'd run out of eggs.' 'She wasn't in.' 'Someone spilt it on me.' 'I called you.'

There are also the inconsiderate things we may do, just because 'we want to' even though we know deep down that they're wrong.

Nobody is perfect. We never will be. We can, however, choose to reduce the things that we do which are selfish, inconsiderate, or wrong.

We're all selfish. We all do things because of 'What's in it for me.' We can learn to change the things we desire from something we want for ourselves, to enjoyment in giving. Maybe not all the time, but more of the time.

We may not get our way, but we'll feel better about ourselves.

'It was the men I deceived the most that I loved the most.'

Marguerite Duras

September 19

Fear

'Through the Jungle very softly flits a shadow and a sigh
He is Fear, O Little Hunter. Hunter, he is fear.'

Rudyard Kipling

'Like one that on a lonesome road
Doth walk in fear and dread.
And having once turned round walks on,
And turns no more his head;
Because he knows, a frightful fiend
Doth close behind him tread.'

Samuel Taylor Coleridge

We all face fear. And the most successful of us, have probably had to face and overcome the most fear.

Fear screams "DON'T" so loudly that we become immobilised. The only way to beat it is to wiggle a toe, to make the first fluttering movements and then jump.

Each little triumph we have enables us to move on to the next. The trick is to have the first tiny triumph and the second and the third. We can only do one at a time. More often than not, if we were to answer the question 'What is the worst thing that can happen?' the worst is not, in all honesty, that bad. We just don't want to face it.

'Real freedom is freedom from fear, and unless you can live free from fear, you cannot live a dignified human life.'

Aung San Suu Kye

'Better to be killed than frightened to death.'

R S Surtees

September 20

Apologies

'An apology? Bah! Disgusting! Cowardly!
Beneath the dignity of any gentleman, however wrong he might be.'

Baroness Orczy

Many people agree with that view. I believe they're wrong. When we have made a mistake, it is far more honourable to admit it. It clears the air and makes it possible to move forward.

Many friends and family members fall out and never speak again because of what he/she did. Strangely that is how they both feel, even though they may want to be reunited.

If there is anyone you haven't seen (but want to) because of what 'they' did. Apologise to them. Even – especially – if it's all their fault. 99% of the time, before you've finished apologising (for the thing you didn't do), they will be apologising too and want to share or take some of the blame. Don't deny yourself a friendship because you are too proud to apologise.

'A man should never be ashamed to own he has been in the wrong, which is but saying, in other words, that he is wiser today than he was yesterday.'

Alexander Pope

September 21

Living

‘An old grandfather of ninety was planting an almond tree. “What Grandad!” Zorba exclaimed, “Planting an almond tree?” And he, bent as he was, he turned around and said, “My son, I carry on as if I should never die.” Zorba replied, “And I carry on as if I was going to die any minute.” ’

Nikos Kazantzakis

How do you live your life? As the grandad, Zorba, or neither?

How do you eat an orange?

Do you pierce the zest and smell it?

Do you feel it exploding in your mouth?

Do you share it with others?

Or do you just eat it?

Or worse still, do you let it shrivel up, or mould, and end by throwing it away.

‘But boldly say each night,
Tomorrow let my sun his beams display,
Or in clouds hide them; I have lived today.’

Abraham Cowley

September 22

Giving

'Giving presents is one of the most possessive of the things we do.... It's the way we keep a hold on other people. Plant ourselves in their lives.'

Penelope Lively

It is so so difficult to give... and to let go.

And yet that is surely what we should do. If we give something away, it is no longer ours. When we give the object, we also give away the right to the object. We no longer have the right to say, how, when, where or even if it's used.

It is true that how the gift is received and used may alter our decisions on whether or what to give in the future, but that is a side issue.

What is important 'now' is to give the things we chose, and give them without strings or expectations. If we give something because we want something in return that is not a gift, it's a bribe.

If we want joy for ourselves and happiness for others, give absolutely freely, with no expectations or demands – delight at being in a position to give and receive blessings at the same time.

'Blessed are those who can give, without remembering, and take without forgetting.'

Elizabeth Bibesco

September 23

God

'How can I believe in God when just last week, I got my tongue caught in the roller of an electric typewriter.'

Woody Allen

'God speaks to us every day, but we don't know how to listen.'

Mahatma Gandhi

If we thank God every day for the challenges and problems in our lives, it will take the sting out of our troubles.

It immediately detaches us from them when we thank God. We move into a different realm, knowing that we are not alone and that by travelling through them we will come to better times.

However bad things are, we will be able to use our present experiences to benefit others in the future,

Thanking God and handing our lives over, opens the gate marked 'Freedom and Joy'. It is there for us to walk through.

'The nature of God is a circle of which the centre is everywhere and the circumference nowhere.'

Empedocles

September 24

Individuality

'It's one of those irregular verbs, isn't it? I have an independent mind, you are eccentric, he is round the twist.'

Jonathan Lynn & Anthony Jay

So comfortable to conform, not to stick out, not to embarrass oneself. And when people do rebel, a little, they believe that their flashing bow tie, their outrageous shirt, their succinct put-downs, make them different, gives them the right to think of themselves as individuals, as special and different.

They may indeed be a little bit different from others, but only in the same way that nearly everybody is a little bit different in some way, however invisible it is.

Real individuality, regardless of how much we may outwardly conform (or not) is when we know and follow our inner being, when we are in touch with the source of life that is within us and will guide us if we let it.

'Ah! from the soul itself must issue forth
A light, a glory, a fair luminous cloud
Enveloping the Earth.'

Samuel Taylor Coleridge

September 25

Crisis

'We have the wolf by the ear; and we can neither hold him, nor safely let him go.'

Thomas Jefferson

'Swimming for his life, a man does not see much of the country through which the river winds.'

W E Gladstone

Some people can make a crisis out of a feather falling. Everything is doom, gloom, and intensity.

Others, a few, remain calm whatever is going on.

If we don't view things as 'the end of the world' we are far better able to cope with the troubles life throws at us.

In reality, in the long run, certainly over two or three lifetimes, very very little is of any significance. That being the case, when someone breaks a cup, smashes our car, or our daughter becomes mysteriously pregnant, if we react calmly, we are likely to be of more support to others, and definitely far greater help to ourselves.

Stress depletes us. Calm restores us.

'There cannot be a crisis next week. My schedule is already full.'

Henry Kissinger

September 26

Principles

'Those are my principles and, if you don't like them.... Well, I've got others.'

Groucho Marx

We behave according to our principles. Or do we? Sometimes we are so ingrained in our habits and behaviours, that we do them without thought.

When we react with superiority, sarcasm, put-downs, racism, sexism, greed, sloth, (to pick a few at random, how many did you tick?) we are no longer acting according to our principles.

If we go inside ourselves, we know what's right and wrong. (Even if we've been doing the wrong all our lives, as did, our parents and our grandparents.)

No one is perfect. None of us are going to get rid of all our faults. However, if we go inside and honestly review our behaviours, we may find some that we are sufficiently distressed by enough that we want to change them.

(We could, later, have another house clean, and another...)

The more we are living by our principles, the more in harmony we will be with ourselves and the world, and the happier we will be.

'It is easier to fight for one's principles than to live up to them.'

Alfred Adler

September 27

Change

'Life is for each man a solitary cell whose walls are mirrors.'

Eugene O'Neill

All about us, those we see, are reflections of ourselves. But the mirrors are from the fairground, and all our reflections are distortions of reality.

The exciting truth is that by ironing ourselves out, by working on our imperfections, we can change the world.

If we go halfway to meet it, it will almost certainly travel the other half, and welcome us. We can discard pretense. We can put out our hand and welcome ourselves into the world.

Some won't put out their hands, and they don't wish to make an effort to interact with us, with equality. And frankly, we are better off without them. The ocean is full of fish, let's find the ones that swim as we do.

'Man's loneliness is but his fear of life.'

Eugene O'Neill

'When one does nothing, one believes oneself responsible for everything.'

Jean-Paul Sartre

September 28

Emotions

'A correspondence course of passion was, for her, the perfect and ideal relationship with a man.'

Aldous Huxley

As we get older, so many of us suppress our emotions. We train ourselves not to cry, not to laugh, not to be vulnerable. We take a deep breath and hold all those emotions in.

And if they do manage to come to the surface – we hide.

"Grown men do not cry!"

To live fully, to enjoy and participate in life, we want to allow our emotions out. Not venting anger, hatred, resentment, but by showing our sorrow, and sharing our laughter, and love, daring to tell others what we really feel.

Rather than trying not to cry, we want to encourage ourselves to weep. Even when we don't find something amusing, we want to encourage as much laughter to bubble out of us as possible. Instead of hiding our feelings by changing the conversation, we want to allow others to understand what we are feeling and experiencing.

The more we do this, the easier it becomes, and the richer our life is.

'The young man who has not wept is a savage, and the old man who will not laugh is a fool.'

George Santayana

September 29

Adventure

'I must go down to the seas again, for the call of the running tide,
Is a wild call and a clear call, that may not be denied.'

John Masefield

Unfulfilled dreams, calling us.

Maybe, oh so quietly now, they've been ignored for so long.

But how long have we got? Might we not flourish if we answered the call.

If we were to abandon the mundane, and travel into adventure, would the world end?

Could it not manage without us?

Discard your shackles. Let the light flood into your dream.

Follow it.

Fulfil yourself.

It's not too late to take a risk.

'You must do the thing you think you cannot do.'

Eleanor Roosevelt

September 30

Imagination

'To travel is better than to arrive.'

Robert M Pirsig

We need to travel. We need to expand our horizons, to have a broader outlook than we have.

Sometimes, in life, we are stuck. There are too many constraints on us. We have nowhere to go. And we cannot go anywhere.

We suffer physically, mentally, and spiritually, because we are, by nature, goal-seeking animals, and we need to continue our journey.

If or when we are physically stuck, whatever the circumstances, we still have our minds.

We can go into our minds and travel to places we have been before, or we can invent places.

Doing this regularly and consistently will make a monumental difference to our well-being. Spiritually, mentally, and probably physically.

All we have to do is do it.

'Coming back to where you started is not the same as never leaving.'

Terry Pratchett

October 1

Temptation

'I never resist temptation, because I have found that things that are bad for me do not tempt me.'

George Bernard Shaw

It may be relatively easy or even challenging for us to resist temptation. For the most part, temptations that we do battle with, at a conscious level, are the ones that are easy for us to identify. Not drinking because we're driving, not having another slice because we want to lose weight, etc. Most of these temptations - as we perceive them are about indulging ourselves.

There is however a swathe of smaller ones, that we hardly notice, may not identify, and which we often give into, without thought.

These tend not to be to do with satisfying ourselves. Instead, they are about our withdrawal from the world or a negative attitude towards it, such as a lack of generosity, pity, concern, or a moment of anger, not bothering to listen or show our love.

We don't recognise them as temptations, they slip in under the radar, and we fail to behave mindfully to those about us – and ourselves.

'His was the sort of career that made the Recording Angel think seriously about taking up shorthand.'

Nicolas Bentley

'I can resist everything except temptation.'

Oscar Wilde

October 2

Action

'They said, "You have a blue guitar,
You do not play things as they are."
The man replied, "Things as they are
Are changed upon the blue guitar."'

Wallace Stevens

We could be so much more than we are if we allow ourselves a little time of self-discovery, and or perhaps self-rediscovery.

Maybe if while we were – travelling to work, waiting for the kids, driving – we contemplated our lives, and considered our day to day behaviour, we might spot places where we could do more or do things differently. And just as importantly, places where we could do less.

If we were to allow space into our lives, we might find ourselves drawn to things that we used to do and have abandoned – because we are so busy!

I don't know what, but you do – gardening, painting, writing, travelling, singing, reading, acting, laughing, walking, cuddling, getting in touch with people, the community, the church.

There is so much more we can do and achieve with our lives, rather than frittering it away with the daily mindless grind.

'Be realistic: Demand the impossible.'

Anon

October 3

Adventures

'Experience is not what happens to a man; it is what a man does with what happens to him.'

Aldous Huxley

'Only when we are no longer afraid do we begin to live.'

Dorothy Thompson

On average, people have seven different careers/jobs during their lives.

Most people fail to save, and yet if their current job paid 20% less than it does, they would be managing with that.

Before going to university, many students take a gap year to gain experience.

If we wait until we retire to have the adventures we dream about, most of us will be too tired or too timid to do them.

If we took a year of retirement and adventure every seven years, we would live far more stimulating lives.

There are always reasons why not to. If we taught our kids what we could, while we spent a year cycling to China, don't you think the kids would come out of it far more enlightened than if we'd all stayed at home, doing the same old, same old.

There are always excuses, like jumps in a horse race. The question is 'What do we do when confronted with a jump?'

'I've looked at life from both sides now,
From win and lose and still somehow
It's life's illusions I recall:
I really don't know life at all.'

Joni Mitchell

October 4

Affirmations

'Every day, in every way, I'm getting better and better.'

Émile Coué

Emile Coué, a French doctor, discovered that getting his patients to say 'Every day, in every way, I'm getting better and better' aloud 15-20 times, morning and evening, vastly improved their health.

The use of affirmations makes an incredible difference to our well-being. Affirmations must be in the present tense, they must be positive, and they must be personal.

Present:- 'I weigh 70 kilos.' (Or whatever weight you want.) If we say, 'I will weigh 70 Kilos' our unconscious hears the word 'will' and thinks well I don't need to do anything about that now.

Positive:- If we say, 'I don't feel shy.' The unconscious doesn't process the negative, it hears 'I feel shy.' And every time we say 'a behaviour', our unconscious 'does' the behaviour. So, if we talk about being shy, fat, insecure, the unconscious relives the process that creates this and reinforces it. So, we want to discard negative words and use positive ones. 'I feel confident.'

Personal:- We cannot make affirmations for others.

It is a good idea to have 2 to 4 affirmations that we use regularly. Repeating them when we're doing something like walking or running is good. 'I feel at ease and confident in all situations.' 'I weigh.... my clothes fit easily.' 'I like myself, I like myself, I like myself.' Saying them aloud and with emotion is better than silently. We are saying things that we want to be true, not necessarily the things that are true now.

'Be very, very careful what you put into that head, because you will never, ever get it out.'

Cardinal Wolsey

October 5

Change

'The feeling of having taken a wrong turning in life was made worse by the fact that he could not, for the life of him, remember having taken any turnings at all.'

Charles Fernyhough

There is one indisputable fact for all of us. We are where we are now. How we arrived here is another matter, but that is in the past, so there is little point going over it.

Tomorrow is another day.

Even if, at the moment, we are unable to change our circumstances, we can choose to view it positively. And, most of us could, if we decided, change our situation.

Doing things that we dislike (or even hate) almost certainly harms us and those around us.

If we are lucky enough to be happy with our lot, there are undoubtedly minor things in our lives that we could do without.

'We all live under the same sky, but we don't all have the same horizon.'

Konrad Adenauer

October 6

Giving

'Morticia Addams "Oh Gonzales – How long has been since we
last waltzed together?"
Gonzales Addams "Hours."'

Anjelica Huston & Raul Julia

Spontaneity.

How long has it been since the last time that you did something beautiful and unexpected for somebody who loves you?

The beautiful and unexpected does not need to cost money.

It does require thought and maybe your imagination.

It is joyous and delightful.

And who amongst us does not like to be delighted and filled with joy?

'We don't really go that far into other people, even when we think we do. We hardly ever go in and bring them out. We just stand at the jaws of the cave, and strike a match, and ask quickly if anybody's there.'

Martin Amis

October 7

Trust

'A man who does not trust himself can never really trust anyone else.'

Cardinal de Retz

Trust starts with ourselves. If we have things that we are hiding from the world, then we cannot be open with others, and we will find it impossible to trust other people. For what we see in ourselves, we see in others.

It does not mean that we have to go confessing our sins to everybody. It means that we need to have cleaned our mental house, discussed everything with at least one other person and learnt to accept ourselves.

When we feel good about ourselves, it is easy to assume the best in others. When we do that, we may be disappointed at times, but our lives will be fuller, and people will find it easier to accept us.

'It is more shameful to doubt one's friends than to be duped by them.'

François Duc de La Rochefoucauld

'He trusted neither of them as far as he could spit, and he was a poor spitter, lacking both distance and control.'

P G Wodehouse

October 8

Inner being

'Thirty spokes share the wheel's hub;
It is the centre hole that makes it useful.
Shape clay into a vessel;
It is the space that makes it useful.
Cut doors and windows for a room;
It is the holes which make it useful.
Therefore profit comes from what is there;
Usefulness from what is not there.'

Lao Tzu

What we are and what we do is important. However, it is our inner soul, our invisible being that matters, that is what makes the difference.

Our journey through life is like a stone being kicked down a street by a small boy until he's bored and then he leaves us in a gutter. It is not where we go or what we hit that should bother us.

We want to take a little time (or even a little more) every day, to stop bouncing around and tend to, nourish and nurture our inner being, and become aware of the peace within.

Not difficult if we do it, impossible to do if we don't.

The angel comes and offers us light and life, and we say 'Yeah but... I'm busy now... how about... tomorrow.'

'The thing that is important is the thing that cannot be seen.'

Antoine de Saint-Exupéry

October 9

Being Alive

' "Why" and "How" are words so important that they cannot be too often used.'

Napoleon Bonaparte

If you've ever done things with children for the first time, their questions flow like bubbles over a waterfall. And the reason they stop asking them is not that the child has all the answers, but because it learns that too many questions are not well received.

And so we, as adults, have that unrequited child within us, still not asking questions, just accepting, and doing – because that is easier.

And that's so sad. It is like taking our most creative friend and putting them into a cardboard box. And so we live in a sterile room because we lack the imagination to transform it.

If our friend has been in the box for too long, it can be difficult to tempt him out. But if we make a real effort, and prize open the box, let a chink of light in, we can start to experience things in a new and enjoyable way.

Just by asking yourself 'Why do we do things that way' – 'Why don't I have pancakes for breakfast?' might be an excellent way to start moving towards a journey of discovery.

'A question is like a knife that slices through the stage backdrop and gives us a look at what lies hidden behind it.'

Milan Kundera

October 10

Tolerance

'Considering all the time you took forming yourself, Elsie, I'm surprised you're not a nicer little girl than you are.'

Noel Coward

It is so easy to concern ourselves with the improvement of others.

So often we know 'how things should be done', and when people do things differently, it can disturb us.

From small things like the way people eat or talk, all the way up to their attitudes, behaviours and beliefs. When theirs don't concur with ours, we want to put them right.

Some people don't care what others do or think. They don't have rules about how other people should do things, they live and let live.

If other people's behaviour does bother us, it is worth taking a step back, allowing them to do things their way, without caring. In the grand scheme of things, does what they do, really matter?

Not caring is amazingly liberating.

'Children with Hyacinth's temperament don't know better as they grow older, they merely know more.'

Saki

"As I know more of mankind, I expect less of them, and am ready now to call a man a good man, upon easier terms than I was formerly.'

Samuel Johnson

October 11

Pause

'I very nearly had to wait!'

Louis XIV

It is so easy to dash through our day, from meaningless action to meaningless event. Never stopping. Just doing. We put one thing down and pick up the next without the blink of an eye.

It is so much better to pause before we start.

To have a few moments of quiet reflection about what we are going to do. And to think about whether it is worth doing, and if it is worth doing, to have a small still space of silence, to meditate, to prepare, to see success, enjoyment and fulfilment.

A life filled with pauses is a more abundant life.

And bizarrely, the more time we spend in contemplative pauses, the more time we have and the more we achieve.

'My heart is at rest within my breast,
And everything else is still.'

William Blake

'He moves from point to point with as little uproar as a jellyfish.'

P G Wodehouse

October 12

Openness

'You come into the world alone and you got out of the world alone, yet it seems to me you are more alone while living than ever going or coming.'

Emily Carr

'I was much too far out all my life
And not waving but drowning.'

Stevie Smith

We adorn the masks we wear with such cleverly detailed intricacies, that for a lot of the time we even fool ourselves.

When we repeat the same fabricated story frequently enough, we come to believe it is true. And it probably had elements of truth woven into it, so it is not surprising that we forget what happened.

Being honest is not only scary, but it is probably nearly impossible.

However, if we want to fully enjoy life, to be able to drink the water from the spring, where it flows straight out of the mountain, rather than the water from the polluted river, if we want that, then we want to start being honest. We want to begin to shed some of our masks.

And when we do drop a mask and discover the world doesn't end, that the gates of hell don't open and swallow us, then we can dare to discard the next one.

We can use our vulnerability to strengthen us rather than enslave and imprison us.

'Courage is not simply one of the virtues but the form of every virtue at the testing point.'

C S Lewis

October 13

Patience

'They also serve who only stand and wait.'

John Milton

When I was young, I worked as a waiter, and I thought that everybody should have to spend a couple of weeks a year working in restaurants or shops, they would then treat the people who are serving them with more respect.

When I got older, I ate in restaurants, and I thought that all waiters should eat in restaurants once a week so that they could learn how to take notice of those they are supposed to be serving.

Then people started phoning me from India to sell me insurance, and I stopped thinking.

It is so easy to be impatient with others when things don't go just how we would like them to.

If we can take a second to put ourselves in their shoes, it is much easier to be tolerant.

And of course, impatience and anger damage us much more than them.

'If you are patient in one moment of anger, you will escape a hundred days of sorrow.'

Chinese Proverb

'His whole attitude recalled irresistibly to the mind that of some assiduous hound who will persist in laying a dead rat on the drawing-room carpet, though repeatedly apprised by word and gesture that the market for the same is sluggish or even non-existent.'

P G Wodehouse

October 14

Insignificance

'Six specks of dust inside Waterloo Station represent – or rather over-represent – the extent to which space is crowded with stars.'

Sir James Dean

Everything to do with us is so important to us!

They are our world. We are the centre of our universe, with our emotions, events, family and everyone else, spinning around us like vast, uncontrollable hurricanes.

And yet if we were able to step back, to view ourselves as a speck of floating dust. Now you see it. Now you don't. It's landed, it's disappeared, we'll never see it again!

What a relief. To feel our troubles just fall away into the invisibility of infinity.

'It is almost impossible to overestimate the unimportance of most things.'

John Logue

October 15

Acceptance

'You must always work not just within, but below your means. If you can handle three elements, handle only two. If you can handle ten, then handle only five. In that way the ones you do handle, you handle with more ease, more mastery, and you create a feeling of strength in reserve.'

Pablo Picasso

It's so easy to stretch ourselves beyond our abilities, or to give up before we start because we don't believe 'We can'.

By accepting that everything is a learning process, (and not a learnt process), we can gradually do more to improve the way we do things. And to improve ourselves, without over-stretching, rather than failing because we do too much, or nothing at all.

Life wants to be fun. Challenges are fun, provided they have the right balance.

It's okay if 'our best' is not 'the best' that it's possible to do.

'The world is made up of people who never quite get into the first team and who just miss the prizes at the flower show.'

Jacob Bronowski

October 16

Rest

'Busy as a one-armed man with nettle-rash pasting on wallpaper.'

O Henry

We all know (hopefully) whether we are morning or evening people. That there are times when we perform better than others.

There are also times during the day when we are up or down.

It is worth keeping a diary for a few days and noting the times when we feel more or less energetic, when our brain is sharper.

If we know the pattern of our ups and downs, we can schedule 'important' things during up moments.

It is a good idea, if it is possible, to take a catnap or siesta during one of the downtimes. It need only be for a few minutes, and it is far better to have a real rest, rather than just filling the time and losing energy, achieving nothing when we're at a low ebb.

'Be a good animal, true to your instincts.'

D H Lawrence

October 17

Boredom

' "What'll we do with ourselves this afternoon?" cried Daisy, "and the day after that, and the next thirty years?" '

F Scott Fitzgerald

Before there was TV, we entertained ourselves!

TV is a sop. A baby's dummy sucked by all.

TV's great advantage is that it requires no effort or even concentration.

That's not to say that TV is useless, just that it is misused mindlessly.

When we do nothing, we have no energy. The more we do, the more energy we have.

How we spend our time is up to us but doing things that require our participation are far more satisfying than being a blob. That's a mental blob and a physical blob.

Be brave! Be daring! Take a risk! Entertain yourself.

'Millions long for immortality who don't know what to do with themselves on a rainy Sunday afternoon.'

Susan Ertz

October 18

Compliments

'Don't waste your life in doubts and fears.'

Ralph Waldo Emerson

Some of us are more confident than others. That's natural. And presumably, most of us would like to be more confident than we are.

Many of us find it extremely hard to accept a compliment. When people say good things to us, or about us, we make a joke about it. We reject it, we go red and wish we weren't there.

We want to accept compliments, say 'Thank you' – while looking the person in the eye – and to believe that the praise is real.

Learning to accept compliments makes a vast difference to our lives and wellbeing.

It is also good to start complimenting and praising ourselves. To say to ourselves, 'You did that really well.' 'That was fantastic – congratulations.' (You needn't do this aloud when there are others there – but doing it aloud when you're on your own is better than doing it silently.)

Put your hand over your shoulder and pat yourself on the back. (Go on do it NOW.) Say, 'Well done'. We all need to be patted on the back far more often than we are.

And start complimenting others whenever you can – and pat them on the back.

'You cannot teach a man anything, you can only help him to find it within himself.'

Galileo Galilei

October 19

Positive thoughts

'I can suck the melancholy out of a song, as a weasel sucks eggs.'

William Shakespeare – As You Like It

How long can we keep sorrow and negative feelings alive?

Indefinitely if we choose, letting so many different memories pop into our minds and ring bell after bell, reminding us to feel bad.

If you've ever walked across a ploughed field with a wellington boot filled with mud and water, you'll know what a stupid thing this is to do, and how much energy it takes.

In the same way, negative feelings/memories require our energy, they drag us down, as we struggle along with them.

We want to release them, wash them away, so that we can live fully in our lives now, unburdened by the past.

How do we get rid of them? As long as we are focusing on them, we will never get rid ot them.

I'm sure you've heard the expression, 'Fake it to make it'. For example, when we pretend to be confident, we become confident.

In the same way, we can decide to stop thinking about the negative and decide to think about something we like. If you had been in a car crash, decide to stop thinking about it and think instead about eating strawberries and cream.

'The moving finger writes; and having writ,
Moves on: nor all the piety nor wit
Shall lure it back to cancel half a line,
Nor all thy tears wash out a word of it.'

Edward Fitzgerald

October 20

Death

Death is nothing at all. I have only slipped away into the next room. I am I, and you are you.'

Rev. Henry Scott Holland

'The dead don't die. They look on and help.'

D H Lawrence

'To die will be an awfully big adventure.'

J M Barrie

Death is with us all. Sometimes close, sometimes remote. But memories and anticipation of it flutter through our minds, however far away it is.

The finality of death is what haunts us, regardless of our beliefs.

If we can allow the idea of, 'I have only slipped away into the next room', it defuses some of the finality. It gives us space to continue to enjoy the company of those who've gone.

And if we are considering our own death, there is one thing that we can be sure of, it is another adventure, and one we cannot avoid. All we can do is leave behind as much love as we possibly can.

'Life is a great surprise. I do not see why death should not be an even greater one.'

Vladimir Nabokov

'It's not that I'm afraid to die. I just don't want to be there when it happens.'

Woody Allen

October 21

Miracles

'There are only two ways to live your life. One is as though nothing is a miracle. The other as though everything is a miracle.'

Albert Einstein

'Some people are born in circumstances which resemble being saddled in the enclosure at Epsom when the race is at Rippon.'

Tom Crabtree

I believe in miracles.

Is winning the lottery a miracle? No.

Is changing from a down-and-out drunk, consumed with self-destruction and utter hatred for the world, to a sober, happy, serene, contributing member of society a miracle? Yes.

On that basis, miracles do happen. The changes do not need to be that extreme for it to constitute a miracle.

To experience miracles in ourselves, we have to stop trying to run the world.

We have to believe that miracles are possible. They require a willingness, energy, great desire, the ability to admit the need for change and the choice to embrace the change.

To experience a miracle, we have to step out of our beliefs into the space where they can happen.

'Where there is great love, there are always miracles.'

Willa Cather

October 22

Senses

'O that 'twere possible
After long grief and pain
To find the arms of my true love
Round me once again!'

Alfred, Lord Tennyson

When we fall in love, we embrace it totally, and we use all our senses. We tell them we love them, we look at them and touch them in special ways. Everything we do and receive confirms our love.

However, we all tend to have one or maybe two primary senses that are the most important to us. If we are verbal, then being told we are loved is the most important. If physical, then being touched means we are loved. If visual, how we are looked at, and how things look are what matter.

As time passes, we tend to use only the sense(s) that are important to us, and tend to stop usigwith the other senses.

So it's entirely possible for people who have been together for a while to no longer know that love is there. 'He doesn't ever tell me that he loves me – so he doesn't love me.' 'She doesn't touch me so much anymore so she can't love me!'

Understanding this, we want to discover what are our partner's primary senses are and use them.

And this does not apply only to one's partner, it also applies to our families, friends, and work colleagues. If we want to bond with people or to influence them, we want to use their senses.

'But love is blind, and lovers cannot see,
The pretty follies that themselves commit.'

William Shakespeare – The Merchant of Venice

October 23

Choice

'Isla Lund: Play it, Sam. Play "As Time Goes By."
Sam: You must remember this,
A kiss is just a kiss.
A sigh is just a sigh:
The fundamental things apply,
As time goes by.'

Ingrid Bergman & Dooley Wilson

Life has its ups and downs. From the ripples on the sea to giant mountain ranges. They all have their ups and downs

And as we travel over them, we can let our oar get stuck in treacle, or we can enjoy the moments of warmth from the sun.

By the end of our day(s), we can have spent more time basking in good moments (or less in bad moments), or we can struggle in the dark molasses.

How we spend today affects tomorrow. The more time we spend noticing the quality moments, the more we'll get. While focusing on gloom, irritation, despair will increase them in our lives.

There will be ups and downs, and we can make both of them either better or worse. It depends on our focus.

'How lucky I am to have something that makes saying goodbye so hard.'

Winnie the Pooh

October 24

Pause

'There was a pause – just long enough for an angel to pass flying slowly.'

Ronald Firbank

Ah, the passing angels. How many we sadly miss – by jumping straight into a welcoming bog.

We live in a world of instant gratification. We not only dash from activity to activity, but many of us speak without thinking.

Cultivating 'a pause' in our life has a multitude of benefits.

It's so hard to retract a statement or an action once it has happened.

And in this age of texting, it's so easy to hurt. Anything in writing can be read and re-read and used to fuel, to inflame the hurt it has created.

Oh for the pause. The moment of quiet reflection. The ability to step back and do nothing.

'He who hesitates is sometimes saved.'

James Thurber

'Time cools, time clarifies; no mood can be maintained quite unaltered through the course of hours.'

Thomas Mann

October 25

Sleep

'I remarked that his eyes were open so he must be awake. "The one on your side is," said the backer, "but the one on the other side is closed. He is sleeping one-eyed." '

Damon Runyon

Ah, Sleep! The restorer of our mind and body. It is good to do whatever we can do help it on its way.

Presumably, you don't drink tea or coffee as your evening leads towards bed. But do you do other things to either assist a good night's rest or at least not make it unlikely?

It's better not to be stimulating our brain with violent or horror movies in the last hour or so of wakefulness. Avoid the late-night news, (we can't do anything about it until morning, except worry, and it may be better by the time we see it tomorrow).

It's good to have a routine of quiet time, prayer, and meditation on our way to sleep, to prepare for sleep and let our unconscious get us ready for the next day. Going over the next day and seeing the successful conclusion of all known events is good. It means that the unconscious understands what we want to achieve.

Enjoy and sleep well.

'The cool kindliness of the sheets, that soon
Smooth away trouble; and the rough male kiss
Of blankets...'

Rupert Brooke 1914

October 26

Self-doubt

'It is easy – terribly easy – to shake a man's faith in himself. To take advantage of that, to break a man's spirit, is devil's work.'

George Bernard Shaw

'Take the life-lie away from the average man, and straight away, you take away his happiness.'

Henrik Ibsen

We don't need others to do this to us. It's so easy to do it to ourselves.

By and large, I don't have vulnerable moments, and most of the time, I would think – that this doesn't apply to me. I am human though, and there are chinks, when self-doubt can poke its head around the door and suck my lifeblood clean away.

Why am I writing these thoughts? All I have to do is have self-doubts, such as – who will read this – and I'm only a small step away from total pointlessness.

Why am I telling you this? Because admitting it is the first step towards ridding myself of it.

Also, I am incredibly grateful to you for the journey of discovery I have undergone, and the adventures I have had because I started to write this for you. Even if you never read it, I feel far richer because of the journey we have been on together. Thank you.

'Man hands on misery to man,
It deepens like a coastal shelf.
Get out as early as you can,
And don't have any kids yourself.'

Philip Larkin

October 27

Thoughts

'Our life is shaped by our mind; we become what we think. Suffering follows an evil thought as the wheels of a cart follow the oxen that draw it. Our life is shaped by our mind; we become what we think. Joy follows a pure thought like a shadow that never leaves.'

Buddha

What we think matters. If we spend our time thinking negative thoughts, hanging out with negative people, putting ourselves down and putting other people down too, it puts the brakes on our life. It turns out the light in our life.

If we choose to focus on positive things, to make the best of the situation we're in, to expect things to be good (even when they're not), we can experience joy.

Even people in situations not of their choosing, a job they hate, prison or refugee camps can rise above the negativity that surrounds them and bring light and hope, not only into their own lives but the lives of those around them.

'When people will not weed their own minds, they are apt to be overrun by nettles.'

Horace Walpole

'The Purple haze, all in my brain
Lately things don't seem the same.'

Jimi Hendrix

'Minds are like parachutes. They only function when open.'

James Dewar

October 28

Addiction

'Years ago, a person, he was unhappy, didn't know what to do with himself – he'd go to church, start a revolution – something. Today you're unhappy? Can't figure it out? What is the salvation? Go shopping.'

Arthur Miller

There are so many things that people use to salve their troubles. Shopping, eating, drinking, watching TV, taking drugs, indulging in porn, playing computer games, gambling, smoking.

We may think that some of them are better or worse than others – certainly, some are more harmful, but leaving that aside – they are all very similar.

Feeling a little stressed, instead of dealing with the cause, we have a cigarette, a cake, a cup of tea, a drink.

'IF', it isn't a problem, if it doesn't harm anyone, ourselves included, maybe it's okay, but probably not.

If we are escaping, then we want to learn how to face up to and deal with our challenges.

We want to discover the root cause of our problems and challenges and deal with them at the source, rather than simply taking or doing something that just dulls the way we feel.

Nobody's perfect. We're never going to be perfect, but maybe we can be better. Perhaps if we were, we would be happier, more enlightened.

'It's a great life if you don't weaken.'

John Buchan

October 29th

Walk

Explore

Look

Discover

October 30

Sarcasm

'If your IQ were any lower, we'd have to water you.'

Anne Robinson

'He's not unlike Hitler, but without the charm.'

Gore Vidal

Sarcasm. Put-downs. Those subtle, clever, remarks, made at the expense of others.

So easy to do, and if we're in the habit of doing them, we hardly notice them.

A form of one-upmanship, of slight superiority or power.

So damaging, so unnecessary.

When people do them to us, we notice their barbs as they enter, although we may think we shake them off, that we don't mind. Sadly at an unconscious level, we do.

If we say them to others, we want to learn to spot them, before they slip out from our lips, and to discard them, unspoken. They damage. If we damage others, ultimately we damage ourselves.

If we find ourselves being bombarded by them, a way of reducing their flow is to question them. Ask people, 'What do you mean by what you've just said.'

'Do you mean that I am an idiot?'

'Do you mean I'm like Hitler?'

By appearing to take what they've said seriously, we take the sting out of the sarcasm. And people will gradually learn to do it less. Hopefully.

'Once a word has been allowed to escape, it cannot be recalled.'

Horace

October 31

Inner Voice

'Dare to know! "Have the courage to use your own understanding," is therefore the motto of the enlightenment.'

Immanuel Kant

There are moments when we hesitate. We may even stumble, crying out that we don't know what to do.

There are times when we do the wrong thing because we have stopped listening to our inner voice – our guide – our guardian.

But deep down, we know what we are meant to be doing. However, we can become very good at switching off, or we bombard ourselves with so many queries that we cannot hear its suggestions.

Of course, drugs, alcohol and sheer willfulness are just a few of the ways to drown out inner knowing easily. And we don't need any of them to ignore it when we want to.

So when we want to know the right thing to do, we need only go inside and enquire. The answer is there.

'Everybody gets so much information all day long that they lose their common sense.'

Gertrude Stein

'The fox knows many things –but the hedgehog knows one big thing.'

Archilochus

Enjoyed?

Share
This
Book
With
Someone
Else

November 1

Self-awareness

'My Mother bores everyone with our photo albums. There's even one called "Pictures We Took to Use Up the Rest of The Film".'

Penelope Lombard

People bore us. But do we bore people? When did we last honestly look at what rubbish we are spouting, or what reaction we are getting?

Unfair – I'm sure you <u>never</u> spout rubbish.

It's easy to talk too much. Many things, our dreams and health, for example, are of no interest to most people.

Suppose we were to challenge ourselves, to find a way to be genuinely interesting to others.... Though in reality that probably means listening to them.... (But surely that's a step too far?)

'Is not life a hundred times too short for us to bore ourselves.'

Friedrich Nietzsche

'A bore is a man who, when you ask him how he is, tells you.'

Bert Leston Taylor

November 2

Gratitude

'Walk as if you are kissing the Earth with your feet.'

Thich Nhat Hanh

'When you are grateful, fear disappears, and abundance appears.'

Tony Robbins

Gratitude, Gratitude, Gratitude, wherefore art thou?

So easy to trundle through the day without gratitude. Or if and when we do feel it, we give it just a cursory nod.

Some people end their day by making a "Gratitude List" – which is lovely, but are they – are you – stopping to experience the full feeling of gratitude?

The best way to experience gratitude is to choose one thing or one person that you feel graterful for and go completely into the feeling, fill your body with the experience of gratitude. Bathe in it. Experience the wonder of the change that flows through you and then take the feeling, the power with you into the next part of your day.

Repeat as often as you want to feel empowered.

'Piglet noticed that even though he had a Very Small Heart, it could hold a rather large amount of Gratitude.'

AA Milne

'[Gratitude] is a sickness suffered by dogs.'

Joseph Stalin

November 3

Happiness

'Happy is the man who, far from business schemes, like the early race of mortals, ploughs and reploughs his ancestral land, with oxen of his own breeding, and no slavish yoke round his neck.'

Horace 65-8 BC

How easy it is to delude ourselves that making that extra money, having that extra thing will make us happy.

We cling to what we have, like rats to a plank from a sinking ship, terrified to let go, when on the other side of the wave, is the shore.

The happiest children I ever saw were playing with a matchbox in the dust outside their hovel, totally absorbed.

Some of the best meals I've eaten have been as a stranger, fed and housed by families living in one-room shacks.

We do not need... In order to be happy

We want to give and share our happiness, enrich the lives of others and ourselves.

We can do this wherever we are and with whatever we do or do not have.

'It is only possible to live happily ever after on a day-to-day basis.'

Margaret Bonanno

November 4

Self-acceptance

'I often think of making geographical change but in my experience it just does not work. If you went to the South Pole, the first person you would meet there would be yourself.'

Jeffrey Bernard

In our moments of unhappiness or disquiet, we may try to run away. The grass is always greener on the other side of the hill, we suppose and/or hope.

Though most of us know this just isn't true. Sometimes, instead of waiting to change location, we convince ourselves that 'if only we... went to the gym... stopped eating biscuits... spent more time in the pub...' everything would change, everything would be alright.

We can't run away from ourselves, so if we don't like the way our life makes us feel, we want to do some soul searching and identify the cause of the trouble and change that.

Sometimes it is necessary to make significant changes to our lives, change our job or relationships. But unless we change ourselves at the same time, we are simply likely to recreate the problems in the new surroundings.

'If you board the wrong train, it is no use running along the corridor in the opposite direction.'

Dietrich Bonhoeffer

November 5

Blame

'The problem is not that there are problems. The problem is expecting otherwise and thinking that having problems is a problem.'

Theodore Rubin

'Well, here's another nice mess you've gotten me into.'

Oliver Hardy

Ah... the Sunday afternoon delight of having problems, something we can really enjoy sinking our teeth into...

How often do we raise a finger – 'I accuse... them... of...' So easy to diminish our involvement, until, after the third or fourth telling, we genuinely believe it was all their 'fault'.

(The fact that we were driving the only moving vehicle when it happened (and incidentally they'd parked and left their car thirty minutes before) doesn't alter the obvious truth that they were totally to blame.)

It is wonderful to be blameless. We really ought to do it more often!

'You can't think rationally on an empty stomach, and a whole lot of people can't do it on a full stomach either.'

Lord Reith

'It is useless to attempt to reason a man out of what he has never reasoned himself into.'

Jonathan Swift

November 6

Sleep

'I have come to the borders of sleep,
The unfathomable deep
Forest where all must lose
Their way.'

Edward Thomas

If you are in bed, and you wish to go to sleep, do not try to write limericks in your head.

~~~

There once was a fellow named Mick
Who could fall asleep in a tick,
Till once as he lay on his side
With his worrisome, mind he tried
To compose a new limerick.

~~~

'What hath night to do with sleep?'

John Milton

'And so to bed.'

Samuel Pepys

November 7

Action

'It is well to remember that the entire universe, with one trifling exception, is composed of others.'

John Andrew Holmes

In the grand scheme of things, we are just statistics. Last year 17% of those living in ... were... One million newborn babies die within the first 24 hours... Somebody disappears in this country every... seconds.

We don't feel like statistics. It's all very personal to us. But that is all we are. And all we will remain unless we decide to do something.

If you and everyone you knew, each held a fundraiser for the charity of their choice, would that make a difference? That would be 100 fundraisers if you knew 100 people.

If everybody they knew did it too... ?

Just a thought. Unachievable.

And yet, if this year just you and I did it, that would make a difference.

And actions, create action, which achieves results.

Where can we go from there?

'No man thinks there is much ado about nothing, when the ado is about himself.'

Anthony Trollope

'I'd always assumed I was the central character in my own story but now it occurred to me I might in fact be only a minor character in someone else's.'

Russell Hoban

November 8

Awareness

'Only in the present do things happen.'

Jorge Luis Borges

It is so easy to pass through our daily lives and just not notice. To take things, people, ourselves for granted. What a sad waste. We only have now, and yet we pass through days, weeks, years without noticing the flower, the cloud, the moon.

We drift along without taking time to listen, to thank, to compliment, to add any value to the existence of others. We can neglect ourselves, our souls, our need for quiet reflection.

Children laugh a hundred times a day, and adults only need their fingers to count their daily laughter.

So decide now to stop for some moments today.

To give time, praise, love to others.

Give time, praise, and love to yourself.

It takes but a moment.

'Eat the present moment and break the dish.'

Egyptian Proverb

November 9

Behaviour

'You cannot step twice into the same river.'

Heraclitus

'If we want things to stay as they are, things will have to change.'

Giuseppe Tomasi di Lampedusa

Life goes on, we cannot stop the river or push it faster. We can put up our hand, but we cannot halt the wind.

We can adjust our sails and sail faster or slower. We may even be able to sail more quickly than the wind, but we cannot stop it.

Good and bad, happy and sad, they all happen, and all we can do is experience them as well as we can.

Following a spiritual path, striving to do the right thing, to be 'good' is no picnic. Being thoughtless, giving in, over-indulging, practicing self-pity are all easy, it takes courage and effort to be true to ourselves.

We may not be able to change the world, but we can change the little bit we do, and the way we do it.

And so we do what we do. We know whether it is right. We go to bed with it, and we get up with it. We can reflect on it or ignore it. It all depends on who we want to be.

'We do not what we ought;
What we ought not, we do;
And lean upon the thought
That chance will bring us through.'

Matthew Arnold

November 10

Change

'The unripe grape, the ripe, and the dried. All things are changes, not into nothing, but into that which is not at present.'

Marcus Aurelius

So many of us become 'stuck in our ways'. We wear the same clothes. We have the same hairstyle, and we eat the same food, we do the same things.

If we can challenge ourselves, to be a little adventurous, maybe change our hairstyle or clothes, wear unusual (for us) colours, when we see ourselves, we would feel different.

When we feel different, we are open to new ideas, and we dare to experiment with experiences.

All we need to do is to be brave. Have a 'make-over', change appearances. Indulge your imagination. Get someone else to make the choices for you. Live a bit!

'His socks compelled one's attention without losing one's respect.'

Saki

'Dress cute wherever you go. Life is too short to blend in.'

Paris Hilton

'Imagination is intelligence with an erection.'

Victor Hugo

November 11

Habits

'There was really no joy in pouring out one's sins, while he sat assiduously picking his nose.'

Ronald Firbank

Now, I'm not saying that you pick your nose (though I must confess that I suspect that you do).

Be that as it may, we all have habits – little habits, most of which we're probably not even aware of.

When we start a relationship – during the first blooms of being in love – everything our partner does delights us. However, after time, some of these things begin to irritate us.

So, if we live or work with others, there are almost certainly things that we do that irritate them.

It is worth asking them what they are and then do our best to change the habit unless there is a genuinely good reason for it. And during the process, we may manage to get other people to alter some of their habits.

And it is worth remembering that if they cannot stop, they are probably not doing things just to irritate us, but because they are locked into their habit.

'Nothing matters very much and few things matter at all.'

Arthur James Belfour

'Rigid, the skeleton of habit alone upholds the human frame.'

Virginia Wolf

'I even hate the way you lick stamps.'

Danny DeVito

November 12

Freedom

'I sit on a man's back, choking him and making him carry me, and yet assure myself and others that I am very sorry for him and wish to ease his lot by all possible means – except by getting off his back.'

Leo Tolstoy

We do this to the ones we love, and we do it to ourselves, and of course, they do it to us. We make impossible demands on each other and stamp our feet when we don't get our way.

Generally, it is 'oh so subtle', so that neither they nor we notice what is happening. There are just 'quiet' expectations about how things should be – followed by disappointment when things do not turn out as hoped.

You may be saying 'I/we don't do that!' to which the question is 'Are you sure?'

Do we grant freedom to others or ourselves? Are we not tied into habits and behaviours, patterns, and outcomes, that rule nearly every aspect of our lives?

Yes, life may be easier like that. It can be more comfortable. (Perhaps.) After all, it requires less effort.

But are those satisfactory reasons?

'Like a bird on the wire, like a drunk in a midnight choir,
I have tried in my way, to be free.'

Leonard Cohen

November 13

Delusions

'How many of our daydreams would darken into nightmares if there seemed any danger of their coming true!'

Logan Pearsall Smith

The distance between daydream and delusion is similar to the length of a piece of string. They can merge into one another. The real problem is that we frequently do not realise that we are deluded.

If we move into delusion about ourselves or life or others, we are in danger. It can be like stepping off a cliff. There is nothing but air to stop us from falling.

It's very important to be watchful, to make sure that we are not so deluded that we believe our delusions to be real. We want to discuss our path and our life with someone we trust, lest we leave the track without noticing.

Our delusions can damage others as well as ourselves.

If we are able honestly to stop acting willfully and to listen to the guidance that comes from within, we can then learn to trust and to discard our illusions, and we can face reality. We can deal with reality. We can triumph.

'What we're saying today is that you're either part of the solution or you're part of the problem.

Eldridge Cleaver

November 14

Prayer

‘We allow our ignorance to prevail upon us and make us think we can survive alone.’

Maya Angelou

I knew a girl who used to wake up in the morning and say, ‘Good God Morning!’ and retreat beneath the covers. She changed her life, now she awakens and says, ‘Good Morning God!’

If at the break of our day we take a moment or three and hand our lives over to the Universal Power, The Light within, God, call it what you will, it can change our day.

We experience peace and calm, a way that we can flow through the day, far better than if we leap up and charge blindly into the next moment, and the next, and the next.

Handing our life over, asking for guidance and listening quietly, rather than dashing around or even just sitting like a blob, is very liberating.

Being grateful for our day, and all the wonders in it, and the opportunities that we have helps us to keep the channel open.

‘Being still and doing nothing are two very different things.’

Jackie Chan

November 15

Possessions

'Spend, spend, spend.'

Vivian Nicholson

(When asked what she was going to do with a record football pools win.)

Most of us have objects in our homes that we've bought, used once, maybe even twice, that now gather dust in a cupboard. How many do you have? 5, 10, 20, more?

And yet when we bought them, we really wanted them. Sometimes we scrimped and saved for ages to get them.

Why do we do this? Repeatedly? Maybe it's because we are focusing on the 'not-having' and the belief that 'it will make all the difference'. We have forgotten that previous purchases didn't 'make all the difference'. And if we haven't forgotten, we convince ourselves that this one is going to be different – because – 'this is the one thing that we really, really need'.

Perhaps if we were to honestly travel forward a couple of months and see the object, not being used, just gathering dust like all the others, we might be able to avoid the purchase. Maybe a better use of our energy would be the disposal of some of our unused possessions.

'The difference between men and boys is the price of their toys.'

Malcolm Forbes

'Few rich men own their property. The property owns them.'

R G Ingersoll

November 16

Joy

'Surprised by joy – impatient as the wind
I turned to share the transport.'

William Wordsworth

Look! Look! Look at that! Look what I've found!

The intense need of the young to share their moments of joy and excitement.

The need is still within us. It is just that we have learnt to suppress it because childish enthusiasm is embarrassing.

Sharing our joy, happiness and achievements with others enriches their lives and intensifies the feelings for us. We want to make a point of sharing our discoveries, successes, and elation with others.

Go on, be brave, allow yourself to become excited.

'Thousands of candles can be lighted from a single candle, the life of the candle will not be shortened. Happiness never decreases by being shared.'

Buddha

November 17

Memory

'Teach us delight in simple things
And mirth that has no bitter springs.'

Rudyard Kipling

We scurry or trudge through our lives, never stopping to notice. And when we look back, what do we remember?

We gobble down our food without savouring its taste.

Whether you live a high speed, event-filled, pack-it-all-in life or are just struggling along with mundane.

How many moments over the last 24 hours have you savoured? How many more could you have enjoyed?

A day, a week, a year from now, what will your memories be?

We can learn to catch so many more memories and enrich our lives.

'Enjoy the little things, for one day you may look back and realise they were the big things.'

Robert Brault

November 18

Dawn

'Morning has broken
Like the first morning
Blackbird has spoken
Like the first bird.'

Eleanor Farjeon

Most of us, most of the time, miss the dawn. It's not on our schedule. It's not in our thoughts.

And yet the dawn is magical. More beautiful, even than the sunset. To add quality to life, to add peace and joy to our existence, at least once this year, let's schedule in a day when we'll rise in the dark, go to the east, and watch.

Watch in silence and wonder, don't let the chatter of life intrude. Give it all your attention, physically, mentally, spiritually. Become totally bathed in the event.

'Down the long and silent street,
The dawn with silver-sandaled feet,
Crept like a frightened girl.'

Oscar Wilde

November 19

Promises

'Promises and pie-crust are made to be broken.'

Jonathan Swift

'In the dim background of our mind, we know what we ought to be doing but somehow we cannot start.'

William James

By and large promises 'to do' things, appear to be made by the receiver of the statement, not the giver. 'She promised she'd tidy her room!'

So it is better not to say we will do things, that we may not do, or have no intention of doing. It only leads to disappointment, sorrow, and angst.

Conversely, people often make promises 'not to do' something, with vehemence, when in fact the promiser is virtually incapable of keeping their promise. Although at the moment of making the promise, they often genuinely believe that they will do it.

'I promise I won't buy any chocolate.' 'I promise I won't see her/him again.' 'I promise on my life that I will never drink again.'

To achieve this sort of promise, we need help. Whether it is a threat of such enormity that it gets through to us 'If you see her again, you will never see your children again.' Or some outside help like therapy or AA.

We want to take care of what we say so that we don't disappoint others or ourselves.

'To promise not to do a thing is the surest way in the world to make a body want to go and do that very thing.'

Mark Twain

November 20

Appearances

'The most common error made in matters of appearance is the belief that one should disdain the superficial and let the true beauty of one's soul shine through. If there are places on one's body where this is a possibility, you are not attractive – you are leaking.'

Fran Lebowitz

'She may very well pass for forty-three
In the dusk with a light behind her!'

W S Gilbert

It is so easy to judge people by their appearances. We make our first impression in the first 10 seconds. At the same time, we are making our first impression on them, so it isn't surprising that we write people off – in ignorance.

What is the first impression that we make? Is it studied or just habit? Might it not be fun to challenge ourselves (and others) by changing our first impression and appearance.

After all, if life isn't fun, what's the point...

'All I say is, nobody has any business to go around looking like a horse and behaving as if it were all right. You don't catch horses going around looking like people do you?'

Dorothy Parker

'It costs a lot of money to look this cheap.'

Dolly Parton

November 21

Soul

'In the greatest confusion, there is still an open channel to the soul. It may be difficult to find because by midlife it is overgrown, and some of the wildest thickets that surround it grow out of what we describe as our education. But the channel is always there, and it is our business to keep it open, to have access to the deepest part of ourselves.'

Saul Bellow

If we have doubts about a soul, let's, just for now, assume that we have one.

If we have one, it resides within us, if ignored for long enough it may shrivel up to the size of a mustard seed, but it's still there.

If we, with peace, allow ourselves to float within, we can find our soul, and we can go into it, we can feel it swell and grow. We can enable it to fill us, to become one with us.

We can radiate its light and power. We can learn to be guided by it.

We can experience wonder and freedom.

(If this is not as easy as we'd like, then we just need to allow ourselves to let go even more, and to become one with it gently.)

'But he that hides a dark soul and foul thoughts
Benighted walks under the mid-day sun;
Himself his own dungeon.'

John Milton

'So the soul, that drop, that ray
Of the clear fountain of eternal day,
Could it within the human flower be seen.'

Andrew Marvell

November 22

Mistakes

'The road to wisdom? – Well, it's plain and simple to express:
Err
and err
and err again
but less
and less
and less.

Piet Hein

That's simple then, we're going to make mistakes – but that's okay, everybody does, as long as we learn from them.

Mistakes are part of the road to growth.

However – if we're a little cunning – we may look at others stumbling about in the dark, spot where the light switch is and use it.

And if we do stumble and bump into things in the dark, there is no point in whacking our shins with a walking stick once the light has come on, just because we made a mistake.

'You must learn from the mistakes of others. You can't possibly live long enough to make them all yourself.'

Sam Levenson

November 23

Decisions

'I have measured out my life with coffee spoons.'

T S Eliot

'Life is not meant to be easy my child but take courage: it can be delightful.'

George Bernard Shaw

Here's an interesting question, 'Why have I chosen this way of life?' Most people go into the – I had no choice – knee jerk answer. Then they think, well maybe I did – but now I'm stuck with it.

And yet... it is undoubtedly the result of the decisions we've taken in the past. And if... we make no new decisions, it will remain much the same.

If we were to consider for a moment (just for fun,) something we might like to change.

Think, for example, how do you write a novel? Only one word at a time. So even if the changes you want to make are small, it's still only one word at a time.

Let's choose one thing that you can begin to do that will start a process of change, and let's be (really really) brave, and begin to do it.

Then perhaps do another, then maybe even the next three, until we reach – Wow!

'Nothing is more difficult, and therefore more precious, than to be able to decide.'

Napoleon Bonaparte

November 24

Tolerance

'When our relatives are at home, we have to think of all their good points, or it would be impossible to endure them. But when they are away, we console ourselves for their absence by dwelling on their vices.

George Bernard Shaw

The mindless smiling prattle of those family occasions, we turn carefully only to expose our good sides, while stifling a yawn.

And yet it is true that blood is thicker than water, and when we find ourselves in difficulties, we may be surprised by how they rally round. Not all of them perhaps, but maybe more than we might have expected.

So perhaps we would enjoy the time we spend with them more if we allowed ourselves to view them more kindly than we sometimes do.

'All my relations are muscle-bound from jumping to conclusions.'

Danny Kaye

November 25

Pain

'Tender-handed stroke the nettle,
And it stings you for your pains.
Grasp it like a man of mettle,
And it soft as silk remains.'

Aaron Hill

Pain is a friend. We have something wrong with a tooth. We get toothache, the worse the pain, the sooner we get it treated. If we didn't get toothache, our teeth would probably just explode, and we would be left with a mouthful of festering stumps.

The trick there was to learn to take action.

Emotional pain is also a friend. It is not an invitation to wallow, to drag ourselves and all about us down. It is an emotional tap (or thump) on the shoulder. 'Something isn't right – please do something about it.'

As with our teeth, we want to fix it as soon as possible, before it grows and festers.

We want to recognise its cause, discuss it with others, and take whatever steps we need to take to change our approach to life so that it can be dealt with and discarded.

'The only thing I regret about my past is the length of it. If I had to live my life again, I'd make the same mistakes – only sooner.'

Tallulah Bankhead

November 26

Smiling

'We are not amused.'

Queen Victoria

Do something for me. You're sitting there reading. Now let the whisper of a smile creep across your face.

You feel lightness. Yes? Not only in your face, but in your being. It feels good.

So simple, yet most of us walk around with 'serious' tattooed on our face, our bodies and minds.

Just for today, or as often as you remember, let that imperceptible smile flutter across your face and through your body.

Check how good it feels. See how much better your day goes. (And if you hit a bad patch, smile a little wider. Jokes are always about disasters.)

Enjoy. Feel Good. Be Happy.

'The reason angels can fly is that they take themselves lightly.'

G K Chesterton

November 27

Listening

'When people talk, listen completely. Most people never listen.'

Ernest Hemingway

Years ago, my boss told me to read 'How to Win Friends and Influence People' by Dale Carnegie. It was written in the 1930s, and I thought, this can't be relevant today.

I also thought 'I know most of this anyway', and I said as much to my boss. 'Yes, I'm sure you do,' he said, 'but are you doing it?'

And when I thought about it, I realised that I wasn't.

For example, we all know we should listen to the people that are talking to us, give them eye contact and our full attention, that we should ask them questions, draw them out and not talk about ourselves.

But do we?

Or are we miles away, or perhaps desperately trying to get in our bit.

How can you watch TV, play a game, or think about all the things you want to say or do and actually listen to what's being said to you?

[Incidentally, 'How to Win Friends and Influence People' is a tremendous book. Read it with a highlighter and go back often to make sure that you are 'doing' it.]

'Oh – I listen a lot and talk less. You can't learn anything when you're talking.'

Bing Crosby

November 28

Disappointments

'Like Dead Sea fruits, that tempt the eye,
But turn to ashes on the lips.'

Thomas Moore

We all have disappointments. As kids, we didn't get the sweet, the trip, the friend we wanted. And on it went throughout our lives.

Now it's work, the football, the wages, our family and friends. They just don't live up to our expectations.

Some of us handle this better than others. Some of us live within a cloud of waspishness, and we talk on and on about how terrible everything is while explaining how wonderful we are.

If we do this, we are just deluding ourselves and adding power to our frustrations.

Let's face it, not everything will work out the way we want. So what! Let's just accept that and enjoy the good things that we do have in our lives. So many people are vastly worse off than we are. This is our one chance at life. Let's enjoy it.

'Some cause happiness wherever they go; others, whenever they go.'

Oscar Wilde

November 29

Love

'My reason will still not understand why I pray, but I shall still pray, and my life, my whole life, independently of anything that may happen to me, is every moment of it no longer meaningless as it was before, but has an unquestionable meaning of goodness with which I have the power to invest it.'

Leo Tolstoy

Without faith and love, we wither and die, like a corpse left on the side of the road.

Love is the food, the water that makes us whole, that enables us to be.

It does not need to be lights exploding, waves crashing, total ecstasy love. It just needs to be human kindness, a hand reaching out. Love simply given and received.

People shuffle and grumble their way through the day, allowing the negatives to suck life out of them.

If we feel that 'nobody loves us', we may be looking for too much, in the unlikely event that nobody does love us, it does not stop us from giving our love, with our thoughts and actions.

'He who wants to do good knocks at the door; he who loves finds the door open.'

Rabindranath Tagore

November 30

Reflection

'Our language has wisely sensed the two sides of being alone. It has created the word loneliness to express the pain of being alone. And it has created the word solitude to express the glory of being alone.'

Paul Tillich

When we sleep, we need to dream, or we become ill.

In the same way, to be whole, we need times of solitude and reflection.

It is easy in the world today to fill every second with mindless distractions. Our lives are cluttered from the moment we wake, until we sleep again. In the past, our ancestors would have had time for reflection, while now we are consumed with TV, phoning, driving, gaming.

It is wise (actually essential – but I don't want to labour the point) to set aside time every week, when we can consider our life, our direction, our loves, our truths. We want to know what it is that we're doing so that we can give it our full attention and bring ourselves back to it when our mind strays. And we want to do this away from any distractions.

It's a good idea to write our conclusions down so that we can see how they change and develop.

Oh, and it is rewarding to add a few minutes of meditation into every day.

'Solitude is for me a fount of healing which makes my life worth living.'

Carl Jung

'Then stirs the feeling infinite, so felt
In solitude, where we are least alone.'

Lord Byron

December 1

Letting Go

'Thus, I live in the world rather as a spectator of mankind than as one of the species.'

Joseph Addison

We can go through our day in our bodies, experiencing everything, or we can step outside ourselves and watch ourselves and others as the events unfold.

We want to be in our bodies when we make love, eat delicious food, gasp at beauty. We want to live those moments fully.

Some things happen that are unpleasant. We get frustrated by other drivers, and we lose it. We fume, delayed at the checkout, behind someone who wants to pay with a jar of pennies. We look on in horror when our child breaks their arm.

If we step out of our bodies and watch the scene, we won't become emotionally involved in it. We won't react in the same way.

It is quite easy to do, simply float out of your body into the corner of the room and look down on yourself and the situation you're in and observe it. You will find that you no longer have the feeling that you had while you were in it.

It is worth practicing this in unimportant situations so that you will find it easy to do when you need to.

People, like paramedics, must spend their working day observing themselves. If they were in their bodies, they wouldn't be able to cope with the horrors they encounter.

'It is not enough to have a good mind; the main thing is to use it well.'

René Descartes

December 2

Resentments

'A man that studieth revenge keeps his own wounds green, which otherwise would heal and do well.'

Francis Bacon

The all-consuming awfulness of the desire for revenge, the total belief that we have been wronged. The replaying in our minds of some 'slight' that we imagine 'they' did to us.

I know people who have taken others to court to try and get a few hundred or even a few thousand pounds they are owed. Yes, that may be a lot of money to them, but the horrendous turmoil that they go through, the way the whole affair poisons their mind and body is extraordinary. I always feel that if you offered them ten times the amount, to endure that degree of stress and suffering, they would refuse. Their own madness blinds them.

Revenge and resentment are things that we want to avoid at all costs. They just consume and destroy.

If people have wronged us, let us forgive them, before we do even more harm to ourselves.

Pray and meditate for them. See them bathed in the Brilliant White Light that is Universal Unconditional Love and Healing. It is not your love. You do not have to love or like them. Just allow yourself to be a channel through which the light can flow.

'Indeed, revenge is always the pleasure of a paltry, feeble, tiny mind.'

Juvenal

'There is no revenge so complete as forgiveness.'

Josh Billings

December 3

Self-acceptance

'I have offended God and mankind because my work didn't reach the quality it should have.'

Leonardo da Vinci

When we were children, many of us felt that if we didn't do things as well as they could be done, that there was something wrong with us.

Not understanding that we were doing things as well as we could, and if we persisted, we would get better. Even when we were encouraged, we frequently failed to hear it.

Some of us have never learnt, that just doing things as well as we can, is okay. We still put ourselves down.

It helps if we can realise that others feel the same way as us. We want to accept our imperfections and go to others who are better than we are and get whatever help we need to improve.

We may never reach perfection. But that's okay, do you know any mortal who has?

'Man's main task in life is to give birth to himself.'

Erich Fromm

December 4

Youth

'I remember my youth and the feeling that will never come back any more – the feeling that I could last forever, outlast the sea, the earth, and all men; the deceitful feeling that lures us on to joys, to perils, to love, to vain effort – to death; the triumphant conviction of strength, the heat of life in a handful of dust, the glow in the heart.'

Joseph Conrad

So easy to forget the passion, the immortality, the joy. Our hearts crying 'Let me live, let me live... '

To anyone who is still there, who still feels this, immerse yourself fully. Treasure every moment.

For the rest of us, if we take a moment now and then to access the feelings we had, to really go into them and relive them as much as is possible, we can re-experience.

Generally, as we recall we go 'Yes, yes, I remember ... ' and we never take the time or the energy to uncover the emotions we experienced.

So now, why not take that memory, go right into it, and feel in your body now, the feelings that you had then. They are the treasured gems we want to hunt for, they will truly reward us.

'Someday, youth will come here and thunder on my door, and force its way into me.'

Henrik Ibsen

Make me young, make me young, make me young.'

Kurt Vonnegut

December 5

Impatience

'Nothing great is created suddenly, any more than a bunch of grapes or a fig. If you tell me you desire a fig, I answer that there must be time. Let it first blossom, then bear fruit, then ripen.'

Epictetus

We live in such an instant world, and we forget that time is needed.

Sometimes we forget this about ourselves and others too. We want things now. We don't realise that we need to allow them to happen at their own speed, and in their own way,

We get frustrated when others don't do what we want them to do. Maybe they are not ready to be 'as perfect' as we are. Ranting about it seldom succeeds. We just have to accept it and allow them to grow (or not) in their own time.

What a relief this can be, to them and us, if we allow ourselves to be patient.

'The rainbow comes and goes,
And lovely is the rose.'

William Wordsworth

December 6

Opportunity

'There is a tide in the affairs of men,
Which, taken at the flood,
Leads on to fortune;
Omitted, all the voyage of their life
Is bound in shallows and in miseries.'

William Shakespeare – Julius Caesar

When I was in my 30s, I was making furniture in a workshop with friends. They decided to reorganise and told me that I would have to leave.

I was devastated and told them that there were two short stories I'd heard on the radio that I remembered.

One was about a verger at a church who couldn't read or write. An incoming vicar sacked him because he couldn't read. The verger took his savings and opened a small tobacconist and sweet shop, it went well, so he opened another.

Years later he was being interviewed by a journalist, who said 'Here you are with hundreds of shops all over the country, worth millions, and you can't even read or write. Can you imagine what you would have achieved, had you been able to?' 'Yes' he replied, 'I'd have been the verger at St Joseph's Parish Church.'

In everything, we do there is the potential for opportunity or disappointment. We are not tied to what is happening. It is up to us.

'Why then the world's mine oyster,
Which I with sword will open.'

William Shakespeare – The Merry Wives of Windsor

December 7

Action

'If only I could get down to Sidcup! I've been waiting for the weather to break. He's got my papers, this man I left them with, it's got it all down there, I could prove everything.'

Harold Pinter

The other short story on the radio that I remember, (in case you've been wondering) is this.

A man was renting a room in a lodging house, all very proper, filled with antiques. In the hall was a beautiful barometer that he looked at every morning as he left.

One day there was a baby spider inside the glass. He watched it grow bigger and bigger. It was trapped and could no longer get out. After much soul searching, he decided that he would break the glass the next morning as he left. Okay, he would have to find new lodgings, but he knew he had to do it.

He came down that morning, ready to do the deed, whatever the consequences and the spider lay curled up at the bottom of the glass, dead.

We are only here once. Don't let's wait until it's too late to do the things that we...

'Could have had class. I could have been a contender.'

Marlon Brando

December 8

Happiness

'Those who are unhappy have no need for anything in this world but people capable of giving them attention.'

Simone Weil

'The secret of being unhappy is to have the leisure to bother about whether you are happy or not.'

George Bernard Shaw

Unhappiness is a 'me' thing. It is focusing on ourselves, our troubles, past mistakes, the unfairness of everything and fear of the unknown future.

It is easy to do, and we just need to have a quiet wallow in any of those to induce unhappiness.

It is as if we are walking along, simply looking at our feet, complaining about our shoes, the mud, the dog shit and the litter. While if we were to look up, we would see the world around us, the view, the breeze scuttling across the field of corn, the gulls diving over the sparkling sea, the multitude of flowers and wonder.

So... if we feel unhappy, we want to take our focus away from ourselves and look out at the world and involve ourselves with others.

'And feel that I am happier than I know.'

John Milton

December 9

Giving

'Ding dong merrily on high
in heaven bells are ringing.'

Traditional

Christmas!

A time for giving, indulgence, fun. A time of togetherness and sharing. A time of wonder and celebration.

Although for many, a time of gut-wrenching loneliness and desolation.

Consider for a moment, if you will, the millions in refugee camps, and those who have to walk two miles for contaminated water. Consider those who are separated from their families, maybe for the first time, soldiers, divorced or separated parents, prisoners, homeless runaway children. Also, those permanently separated from the main society, the tramps and beggars, the cardboard city dwellers.

Think for a moment of the money you are spending and receiving this Christmas. Think about the time spent sitting on the sofa complaining about what is not on TV.

Think if there is something you could give, this and every month. Or whether you might enjoy your Christmas more if you were to help out in a soup kitchen?

'Come away; poverty is catching.'

Aphra Behn

'Oh! God! that bread should be so dear.
And flesh and blood so cheap!'

Thomas Hood

December 10

Greed

'Man is the only animal whose desires increase as they are fed; the only animal that is never satisfied.'

Henry George

Greed makes us prisoners. It ties us down to material things, and it is a rock that blocks a path to spiritual freedom.

Greed goes beyond wanting to 'keep up with the Jones' it wants to 'overtake the Jones'.

There is a vast range to greed, anything from a molehill to a mountain but focusing on a molehill can be all it takes to prevent spiritual progress.

There is joy in greed – and that is greater greed.

It is possible to disguise greed as rational thought, as 'planning for the future,' but it is still recognisable as self-seeking, self-clutching greed.

Greed turns people into liars and thieves, who justify their actions as they pursue the spiral of their obsessions.

Letting go is difficult, but not impossible, and the rewards are genuinely delightful.

'If we command our wealth, we shall be rich and free; but if our wealth commands us, we are poor indeed.'

Edmund Burke

'There is no wealth but life.'

John Ruskin

December 11

Awareness

'Pretentious? Moi?'

John Cleese

We've all watched shows on TV with people behaving thoughtlessly towards others. It's what makes us laugh.

And yet so often things that we find amusing are just variations of our behaviour.

Are there things that we do or say to those closest to us, without even thinking. Could it be that we are behaving with the same embarrassing thoughtlessness that we watch on TV?

The people we are rudest to, take the most advantage of, or ignore, are those closest to us. We wouldn't dream of behaving that way with people we didn't know.

How can we find out if this is what we do? Be mindful and ask them. And if we ask, and don't like what we hear, we need to remember not to punish.

'He was like a cock who thought the sun had risen to hear him crow.'

George Eliot

'May you always know the truth and see the lights surrounding you
May you always be courageous, stand upright and be strong
And may you stay forever young.'

Bob Dylan

December 12

Expectation

'Blessed is the man who expects nothing, for he shall never be disappointed was the ninth beatitude'

Alexander Pope

How sad to go through life expecting nothing.

How much worse though to go through life expecting failure and unwanted outcomes, for yourself or your children, family and friends.

'I'm no good at...' 'She always gets lost.' 'He's always late.' 'I never know what to say.' 'I always feel left out.' 'Everyone else is brilliant at...' (Please add your own)

Is that what you want? To go through life, expecting a second-class existence?

No?

Well, don't say it then.

The unconscious listens to everything it hears and does it's best to make that come true.

'I'm no good at....' the unconscious hears that and says, 'Oh, I can make sure that you make a mess of that.'

So if you don't want something – DON'T SAY IT. Learn to say what you do want.

Watch the 'new' begin to unfold.

'It is never too late to be what you might have been.'

George Eliot

December 13

Behaviour

'It was no wonder that people were so horrible when they started life as children.'

Kingsley Amis

People do not always get their own way. And nor do we. And when we don't get our way, generally we don't like it.

The reaction can take many forms if we think back to how kids behave when they don't get what they want. Rage – sulk – stamp and cry, "It's not fair."

Whatever the child's strategy was – and it may have worked then – it was a childish strategy and should have been discarded with childish things.

What is extraordinary is that so many adults continue to use the same strategies now.

If they do, and providing they're not your boss, you may be able to get them to change to a better way of behaving by telling them that you are no longer going to react. And refuse to respond to their childish outbursts.

If we are the culprits ourselves, then it behoves us to take this opportunity to grow up and start behaving with maturity.

'There is only one cardinal sin: impatience. Because of impatience, we were driven out of Paradise; because of impatience we cannot return.'

Franz Kafka

December 14

Change

'In my end is my beginning.'

Mary Queen of Scots

'In my beginning is my end.'

T S Eliot

Most of us probably don't think much about compost, the fact that last year's meals have turned into this beautiful friable earth, full of nutrients.

And yet everything is either growing or dying. Everything is always changing.

This is true of events and people and personalities.

The only constant in life is change. It's our common bond.

We so easily fall into the trap of the importance of the events we are in, feeling that they are far greater than they are.

What happens now, what people think about it, or us, soon will not matter.

If we can accept everything as being part of the change that we are in, the self-imposed, unrealistic pressures disappear. Understanding this gives us freedom to travel on, through the highs and lows, without being surrounded by a pall of disaster.

'The slow one now will later be fast
As the present now will later be past
The order is rapidly fadin'
And the first one now will later be last
For the times they are a-changin'.'

Bob Dylan

December 15

Persistence

'Nothing in the world can take the place of persistence. Talent will not; nothing is more common than unsuccessful men with talent. Genius will not; unrewarded genius is almost a proverb. Education will not; the world is full of educated derelicts. Persistence and determination are omnipotent. The slogan 'press on' has solved and always will solve the problems of the human race.

Calvin Coolidge

Easy-ish to do when we're up. Hard to contemplate when we're down.

And yet, hauling oneself out of bed, and getting on with it, even when one can hardly bear to, is what makes the difference.

And knowing that other people, other successful people, have overcome enormous trials, is a great help. If only one can remember to process the fact.

'Keep right on to the end of the road,
Keep right on to the end.
Tho the way be long
Let your heart be strong,
Keep right on round the bend.

Harry Lauder

'The drop of rain maketh a hole in the stone, not by violence, but by oft falling.'

Lucretius

December 16

Abilities

‘ “Golden hands he’s got,” said his Father gloomily. “A pianist’s hands. Or a surgeon’s hands.”

“Both,” said his Mother. She blew her nose fiercely. “He could have been both. Operating by day, by night playing Bach.” ’

Alan Coren

Most of us have great abilities, but sadly, by and large, we do not fulfil them. We sometimes think of what might have been and then drift on down the river of life.

And maybe we’ve wasted opportunities, but it isn’t too late to learn, to choose something and move towards it, embrace it with energy and thrill.

We may never become a concert pianist, but that doesn’t mean we can’t enjoy playing.

We just want to start, to nurture something that we can do, or want to do, and little by little, enjoy getting better at it, even on the days when we don’t feel like it.

We’re all good at doing something, even if the thing we’ve excelled at is doing nothing. We’ve made doing nothing an art form. All we want to do now is to redirect a little energy. Enjoy being in the sunshine of living.

‘My only regret in life is that I am not someone else.’

Woody Allen

‘Of all the things I’ve lost, I miss my mind most.’

Ossie Osbourne

December 17

Resolutions

'No bird soars too high if he soars with his own wings.'

William Blake

Another year has gone, with successes and failures, with triumphs and mediocracy. A new year is coming. Will anything change?

So many resolutions hit the scrap heap before they even get out of bed – just idle words and thoughts, with no intention of success.

To aim, expect or hope to do something new, forever, or even for a year or a month, is too long. We may, in our heart, hope that it will last, but if it is to continue, it has to survive today.

We can choose what we do with the next few moments.

When we deny ourselves something, that thing may then become an obsession, for example, no more chocolate cake. We and our unconscious will scheme and plan and use all available cunning until we have a slice. And then, we give in and fail. Chocolate cake is back on the agenda.

It is better to decide, 'I will only eat chocolate cake on the 21st of the month'. Then when we really crave it, we can say 'No, I'm waiting until the 21st', and when the 21st comes, we can choose whether we want any or not.

'Finality is death. Perfection is finality.
Nothing is perfect. There are lumps in it.'

James Stephens

December 18

Arguments

'Discussion is an exchange of knowledge; argument is an exchange of ignorance.'

Robert Quillen

Some people waste so much time and energy fruitlessly arguing, stamping their feet, to get their own way, or to change a closed mind.

When we see other people arguing about things that don't interest us, we wonder why they bother.

Some people don't argue, they just sulk, which is just arguing in silence.

Disagreement is a negative drain. Is it so important that people think like us, or do what we think they should?

If we believe in things strongly and want to change the world, shouting at it does not work. If it did, it would have already changed. We need a new approach.

'In most instances, all an argument proves is that two people are present.'

Tony Petito

'No matter what side of an argument you are on, you always find some people on your side that you wish were on the other side.'

Jascha Heifetz

December 19

Procrastination

'Procrastination is the thief of time.'

Edward Young

I could have written this some other time or tomorrow, so I chose to do it straight away.

How easy it is, not doing.

And yet not doing takes up so much time. Not only the time it takes to finally do it, but all the time consumed deciding not to do it, not to mention the time(s) we spend feeling bad about not having done it, or the time(s) we waste making excuses.

It's just that we never thought about it like that.

Apart from making a decision 'now' not to put things off anymore, a good idea is to schedule what you are going to do into a diary, and then keep your appointment to do them.

Another essential tool is the word 'No', followed by 'I'm not going to do that.' Learning to say that we are not going to do things is vital. There are masses of things that we say we will do, that we have virtually no intention of doing. It is far better to disappoint people once, rather than to keep breaking our promises, and draining our energy.

'Only put off until tomorrow what you are willing to die having left undone.'

Pablo Picasso

December 20

Lending

'If there is anyone listening to whom I owe money, I'm prepared to forget it if you are.'

Errol Flynn

Lending and borrowing can easily and often does end in disaster. So why do it?

If we borrow anything, it is beholden unto us to return it, to return it soon, and not wait to be asked, whether it's a pen, a book or £1,000 we want to take responsibility for returning it, in good condition, as soon as possible. If the book looks as if it's been through a lawnmower when we've finished reading it, we want to replace it with a new one.

None of that, however, is the reason for this writing. It's all about lending, or rather not lending.

If it is at all possible, do not lend anything to anyone, give it to them. Explain that you do not want it back. It is up to them to pass it onto the next person.

If you can't or won't do that, it is better not to lend it to them.

If you give (lend) someone £1000, or whatever it is, the deal is that when someone comes to them to borrow money, they, in turn, pass the money on. It is your responsibility to explain this to them, as you make the gift.

Give, and receive freedom, peace of mind and joy.

'Neither a lender nor a borrower be:
For loan oft loses both itself and friend.'

William Shakespeare – Hamlet

December 21

God

'Operationally, God is beginning to resemble not a ruler but the last fading smile of a cosmic Cheshire Cat.'

Julian Huxley

Somebody said to me the other day – "It's not that I don't believe in God, it feels as if God doesn't believe in me."

In current times, many people have moved away from God and belief, but at times of turmoil, they want something above and beyond themselves.

One of the challenges is that if we have had no belief or contact with God when life was okay, we simply don't know what to do when faced with troubles. We may want to 'turn to God' 'Whatever the hell that means' but when we turn, all we find is emptiness. We may pray, but we find ourselves 'questioning if there is anything to pray to, or believe in.'

It would seem though, that God 'whatever that is' lies within us. If we go into ourselves, into the stillness within, and allow the turmoil to fall away, we can receive strength, peace, and courage far greater than we can normally access.

We can, of course, go within at any time. And in fact, the more often we do, when we are already in harmony with ourselves, the easier it will be when we are troubled.

'You see many stars in the sky at night, but not when the sun rises. Can you, therefore, say that there are no stars in the heavens during the day?'

Sri Ramakrishna

December 22

Kindness

'I shall pass through this world but once. If, therefore, there be any kindness I can show or any good thing I can do, let me do it now; let me not defer or neglect it, for I shall not pass this way again.'

Stephen Grellet

Most of us probably think of ourselves as being kind and given a choice would probably choose to do the kind thing.

How often, though, do we deliberately go out of our way to do something kind? How often do we think 'I will go and do that, it would be kind'?

If we make a conscious decision to do something kind for someone, and do it, not only have we done something good for them, we have also done something good for ourselves.

Every time we do anything that makes us feel good, we are more likely to do it again. And so, we help to grow the sum total of human kindness.

'I have always depended on the kindness of strangers.'

Tennessee Williams

'Kindness is in our power: even when fondness is not.'

Samuel Johnson

December 23

Self-awareness

'If you see anybody fallen by the wayside and lying in the ditch, it isn't much good climbing into the ditch and lying by his side.'

Dick Sheppard

Someone was on their way to visit me the other day and called for directions. 'Where are you?' I asked. He didn't know.

If we don't know where we are, we cannot get to our destination. Firstly, we have to find out where we are.

If we are unhappy and wish to become happy, we have to know who we are now, before we can move on and become the person we want to be. Often, in our state of discomfort, we do not wish to explore it.

To discover our troubles, it is possible to go into the silence within and to explain to the silence that we do not like how things are. To move on, discard our pain, move from darkness into light, we make a decision to change our focus from the negatives thoughts that preoccupy us, to positive ones.

It may take practice and perseverance, but it's worth it and it works.

'Man needs difficulties; they are necessary for health.'

Carl Jung

'A fool often fails because he thinks what is difficult is easy.'

John Churton Collins

December 24

Friends

'Should auld acquaintance be forgot,
And never brought to mind?
For the sake of Auld Lang Syne.'

Robert Burns

We probably sing this (or something like it) in the first few moments of the new year and then – we forget about it. We erase it from our minds.

When we sing that, we're committing to keeping in touch with people. But do we?

For most of us, the answer is seldom or never. And yet there are people whom we've travelled with, that we've abandoned.

If we were to contact some person we've discarded and see them, we would almost certainly bring light into their life, and quite possibly into our own.

A visit, unexpected or expected, is a beautiful thing to receive. Distant friends or relations, you choose. Take a little unexpected time into their lives.

'Not many sounds in life, and I include all urban and all rural sounds, exceed in interest a knock at the door.'

Charles Lamb

December 25

Oneness

'Whatever you do in life will be insignificant, but it is very important that you do it.'

Mahatma Gandhi

'Sometimes I feel like a Motherless child a long way from home.'

Negro Spiritual

You have better odds for winning the lottery than you had for being born.

So make no mistake, you are special. You are very, very important. You are part of the whole, and as such your existence and the things you do, send ripples throughout the world.

There are times when we feel insignificant, or it feels as if everything is conspiring against us. But we want to accept these moments and move on to the next. We don't understand our significance any more than a dab of paint can realise its importance in a painting. But take it away, and the dab before, and the dab before and you'll end up with nothing.

We want to be proud to be that dab of paint, we want to shout and wave our arms and be the best we can be.

'How little do we know that which we are!
How less what we may be.'

Lord Byron

December 26

Courage

'Each time a man stands up for an ideal, or acts to improve the lot of others, or strikes out against injustice, he sends forth a tiny ripple of hope, and crossing each other from a million different centres of energy and daring those ripples build a current which can sweep down the mightiest walls of oppression and resistance.'

Robert Kennedy

Sometimes – maybe even quite often – it can be so much easier to say nothing. We see something happening, and rather than sticking our neck out, we hide behind 'For God's sake, don't say anything!', and pretend not to be involved.

So easy to do, so understandable, so cruel and unworthy.

Everything impacts on all of us, so if we don't play our part when the call comes, then it will have effects in our lives too.

Whatever we do sends out ripples, sets examples, reinforces our behaviour and creates behaviours in others, so we want to make sure that the things we are doing, are the right things – even when they are the harder ones to do.

Let's have courage. Let's be proud of ourselves.

Don't fall into the trap of pretending that it's nothing to do with us, or that we 'didn't really know what was going on', so perhaps it's better to do nothing.

'Only ignorance! How can you talk about only ignorance! Don't you know that it is the worst thing in the world next to wickedness.'

Anna Sewell

December 27

Choice

'Surprised by joy – impatient as the wind I turned to share the transport.

William Wordsworth

Blink and you've missed it.

Our lives whizz by, and we want to be ever vigilant, ready, prepared to grab whatever wonders may come our way today.

It is so easy to allow the swamp of the mundane to drown us, to fail to breathe in the scent of the honeysuckle, to hear the birds first song in the spring, to miss the new moon.

However dark the moment, we are surrounded by light. Where we focus is up to us.

'You only live once, but if you do it right, once is enough.'

Mae West

'To live is the rarest thing in the world. Most people exist, that is all.'

Oscar Wilde

December 28

Patience

'It is very strange.... That the years teach us patience; that the shorter our time, the greater our capacity for waiting.'

Elizabeth Taylor

'Adopt the pace of nature, her secret is patience.'

Ralph Waldo Emerson

How wonderful it is to arrive at patience.

It is a gift to be able to be patient, and not get wound up – but the chances are that if we feel we are being taken advantage of, treated with disrespect, sooner or later we may snap.

So while enjoying our patience, it is essential to monitor any underlying disquiet, and do something about it, before it erupts.

'Beware the fury of the patient man.'

John Dryden

'I am extraordinarily patient, provided I get my own way in the end.'

Margaret Thatcher

December 29

Adventure

'People who dance are considered insane by those who can't hear the music.'

Friedrich Nietzsche

There is a little madness in all of us, but as time goes by we tend to squash it out of ourselves because of the way other people react to our daring.

Without any daring or a little madness, our lives become grey and subdued.

Sadly, we often don't notice the greyness, we accept it as the norm, and if unchallenged, greyness gets darker and darker.

Don't wait until you're retired and too tired to do the things you always meant to do.

Be brave, be adventurous. Dare yourself to have some unbridled fun.

Choose something to do in the next seven days that you have never done before.

And do it.

Dare to be mad.

'I don't suffer from insanity, but I enjoy every minute of it.'

'Senator' Ed Ford

December 30

Light

'Thou art my light; if hid how blind am I!'

Francis Quarles

'We can easily forgive a child who is afraid of the dark; the real tragedy of life is when men are afraid of the light.'

Plato

This a Doing – Not a Reading.
(Though you will have to read it, to do it.)
Get Comfortable.
Ground yourself into the earth.
Close your eyes.
Breathe long and slow.
Put your hands on your heart.
Go into the light in your heart.
Breathe into your heart, the peace, the light.
Let the light and the love spread slowly throughout your body and then out of you, way, way out.
Feel, become one with the stillness, the light, the love, the peace.
Make a mental bookmark to this place, this feeling, this being.
Breathe long and slow and know that you can return here whenever you want to.
All you ever have to do is decide that you are returning to the light and peace, as you take a long slow breath.

'Learn to light a candle in the darkest moments of someone's life. Be the light that helps others see; it is what gives life its deepest significance.'

Roy T Bennett

December 31

Superiority

'Jehovah's Witnesses, awaiting the Last Day with the quiet kind of satisfaction that a man gets in the dry season when he knows his neighbour's house is not insured against fire.'

Bernard Levin

People think they're better than other people. However low a person goes, there is always someone, in his madness, that he can look down on.

Perhaps even truer of the believers in 'their own' religion. They know that theirs is the only way.

What is it about mankind that forces us to create such ideas?

An oak tree doesn't feel better than a nettle. The cheetah and the gazelle do not feel superior to one another. They race, they win or lose, but that's it, that's just the way it is.

The moment we feel special, better, more worthy than others, we are cutting ourselves off from truth.

'Imagine that you are creating a fabric of human destiny with the object of making men happy in the end, giving them peace and rest at last, but it is essential and inevitable to torture to death only one tiny creature... and to found that edifice on its unavenged tears, would you consent to be the architect on those conditions.'

Fyodor Dostoevsky

Made in the USA
Las Vegas, NV
03 December 2022

60987149R00213